D1560003

THE
LIFE
AND
DEATH
OF
LATISHA
KING

THE
LIFE
AND
DEATH
OF LATISHA KING

A CRITICAL

PHENOMENOLOGY

OF TRANSPHOBIA

GAYLE SALAMON

NEW YORK UNIVERSITY PRESS

New York

NEW YORK UNIVERSITY PRESS
New York
www.nyupress.org

References to Internet websites (URLs) were accurate at the time of
writing. Neither the author nor New York University Press is responsible
for URLs that may have expired or changed since the manuscript was
prepared.

LIBRARY OF CONGRESS CATALOGING-IN-PUBLICATION DATA
Names: Salamon, Gayle, author.
Title: The life and death of Latisha King : a critical phenomenology of
transphobia / Gayle Salamon.
Description: New York : New York University Press, [2018] |
Series: Sexual cultures | Includes bibliographical references and index.
Identifiers: LCCN 2017034134| ISBN 9781479849215 (cl : alk. paper) |
ISBN 9781479892525 (pb : alk. paper)
Subjects: LCSH: King, Larry, 1993–2008. | Transgender people—
United States—Case studies. | Murder—United States—Case studies. |
Gender identity—United States. | Sexual orientation—United States. |
Transphobia—United States. | Homophobia—United States.
Classification: LCC HQ77.8.K56 S25 2018 | DDC 306.76/8—dc23
LC record available at https://lccn.loc.gov/2017034134

For Latisha

Except perhaps in the case of some wretched souls who think only of winning or of being right, all action and all love are haunted by the hope for an account which will transform them into their truth—the coming of the day it will finally be known just what the situation was.

—Merleau-Ponty, "Indirect Language and the Voices of Silence"

CONTENTS

INTRODUCTION

I. WEDNESDAY MORNING

On February 12, 2008, Larry King was shot by Brandon McInerney, a fellow student at E. O. Green Junior High School in Oxnard, California. Brandon shot Larry twice in the back of the head at point-blank range with a handgun, one of several kept in the family home. Larry died in the hospital the next day.

> ASSISTANT DISTRICT ATTORNEY MAEVE FOX: [Brandon's] father drove him to school the morning of [the shooting]?
>
> DR. HOAGLAND, EXPERT WITNESS FOR THE DEFENSE: Yes.
>
> FOX: And didn't he, was it was hard to get the gun with his father in the house and he was waiting for an opportunity to get the weapon?
>
> HOAGLAND: Yes.
>
> FOX: And they were hurrying and he almost forgot it and he had to go back into the house and get the gun?
>
> HOAGLAND: Correct.
>
> FOX: It was already loaded with six bullets?
>
> HOAGLAND: Yes.
>
> FOX: Did he recognize that the bullets were hollowpoints?
>
> HOAGLAND: Well he just ran in quickly and grabbed it.
>
> FOX: He almost forgot it?
>
> HOAGLAND: Yes.

FOX: And had to run back in and get it?

HOAGLAND: Yes.

FOX: Because he was going to shoot Larry King?

HOAGLAND: Yes. That was his consuming thought.

FOX: When he got to school, Anton G. asked if he had brought it and the defendant lied and said he had not?

HOAGLAND: Yes.

FOX: And he said English had started in another classroom?

HOAGLAND: Correct.

FOX: During that time he took that gun he had wrapped in a towel and moved it into the front pocket of his sweatshirt?

HOAGLAND: Yes.

FOX: He said his action was unseen because he sat near the back and because the gun was the size of his hand and he had it wrapped in a towel?

HOAGLAND: Correct.

FOX: And these were all things he did to prevent anyone else from seeing the gun?

HOAGLAND: Yes.

FOX: Wrapped it in a towel put in his backpack so his father [could not see]. He did not just walk out waving a gun and say "I'm going to shoot someone." He wrapped it in a towel and secreted it. In fact he told you that he thought of shooting Larry King in classroom 22 but "I could not bring myself to do it. I was never able to get to the point where I was."

HOAGLAND: Correct.[1]

Assistant District Attorney Fox's line of questioning attempted to establish the fact that this killing was not done rashly, that it was not the result of a dispute or an argument, not a decision that occurred in the heat of the moment. Brandon had been planning the killing, and telling people about his intentions, for days beforehand. He picked out the gun from several kept in the family home. He took pains that it not be seen, first hiding it from his father and later from his teachers and classmates at school. He waited, holding the gun in the front pocket of his hoodie, for twenty minutes. There was no sign that he was agitated, no sign that anything was wrong, until he stood up from his seat and fired one bullet, and then another, into the back of Larry's head.

o o o

I first heard about this case, as many people did, from a cover story in *Newsweek* a few days after the shooting. That story, "Young, Gay and Murdered in Junior High: A Tale of Bullying, Sexual Identity, and the Limits of Tolerance," portrayed the killing as a phobic reaction to a gay crush gone bad. Larry had asked Brandon to be his valentine, the story went, and Brandon killed him in a homophobic rage. This narrative of the murder, one of a gay boy's unrequited love for a straight boy, has proven remarkably persistent in characterizations of this case, and when the case reemerges in the media it often appears around Valentine's Day, two days after the murder occurred, in op-ed pieces that argue the need for tolerance of all kinds of love. An off-Broadway play based on the case was titled, simply, *Valentine*, and imagined the two principals as young lovers and the murder as the consequence of romance that had soured. And Marta Cunningham's documentary about the case, which premiered on HBO in 2013, takes its name from the address of the cemetery where Larry King was buried, *Valentine Road*. As a synecdoche for this story, "valentine" appears to be too overdetermined a signifier to resist. In this book,

I will suggest that we *should* resist it—that we should try to see what gets covered over and rendered illegible when the case is described as a crush gone wrong, and will offer a different way of reading, and understanding, what happened in that classroom. It is not that I think we should be wary of the sentimentalizing connotations of the word "valentine," though reading this as a love story with a bad ending achieves that work of sentimentalization quite neatly. The real danger in the valentine-ization of this story is that it uses a familiar narrative of sexual orientation to obscure and ultimately erase a less-familiar one about gender expression. This substitution, I will argue, was consequential in the subsequent murder trial.

I attended that murder trial, which commenced in June of 2011 and lasted for nearly two months. Over the course of that trial, it became clear to me that the story I had been primed to hear, a story about a gay child with a crush on a straight one who then killed him, was not in fact an accurate description of what had transpired. When the trial ended two months later, I became convinced that this was not a story about a gay child and a straight child. It slowly became clear to me that the story of the killing of "Larry King," and the story of the prosecution of that killing, was not primarily about sexual orientation at all but was in fact about gender expression. As a result, the "limits of tolerance," as the *Newsweek* cover story put it, should be understood in markedly different ways.

Much of what happened during this trial hinged on a confusion between gender identity and sexual orientation. The defense in this murder trial presented a challenge to Assembly Bill 1160, a California law banning "gay panic" defenses, in which an ostensibly straight man alleges he was led to attack or kill his gay victim because the victim subjected him to a sexual advance that blinded him with revulsion and rage. In the trial, it became clear that Brandon's murderous rage toward Larry was being described as a defense, not of Brandon's person or body, but of the integrity of his sexual identity. The "gay panic" defense that Brandon's lawyers mounted, in defiance of AB 1160, showed no evidence of explicitly sexual aggression on Larry's part, but relied on a submerged logic in which no sexual provocation was required to provoke such a panic *because Larry's feminine gender was already a panic-inducing provocation.* What we see in this case, and in many instances of violence against gender-nonconforming and transpeople, is that violence justifies itself by characterizing non-normative gender as itself a violent act of aggression and reading the expression of gender identity *as itself a sexual act.*

Throughout this book, I am drawing a crisp distinction between gender identity and sexual orientation, for reasons which will I hope become clear. It is important to note, however, that this is not the only way to think about their relation. Philosopher Talia Bettcher, for instance, has recently proposed a theory of "erotic structuralism," that uses phenomenology—understood as describing the ways that our sexual experiences *feel like* something—to underscore the necessary enmeshment, if not co-constitution, of these categories.[2] This claim that in sexual relation self and other are necessarily gendered offers one way to see these categories as more blurred than we often do. At the same time, Bettcher is writing against some of the more transphobic conflations of gender and sexuality historically offered within the psychological literature. Her argument is complex and compelling, and gives us reason to pause before cordoning gender and sexuality into separate categories. My question here, however, does not inquire into how we feel our gender and our sexuality, but rather asks how those things are read by others. In particular: What are the social, legal, and ethical consequences that result from conflating one with the other? One of the consequences in this case, I hope to demonstrate, was that gender expression was interpreted as a form of sexual aggression.

II. LATISHA

FOX: Once they got there [Brandon] sat where he was supposed to sit?

DR. HOAGLAND, PSYCHOLOGIST CALLED BY THE DEFENSE AS AN EXPERT WITNESS: Yes.

FOX: He didn't remember that Larry King was called into the office?

HOAGLAND: Yes.

FOX: Perhaps because of Larry's brief absence he was able to say "I feel nervous about it because I wasn't sure I wanted to do it."

HOAGLAND: Yes. He thought of no particular consequences.

FOX: He told you "I started to WORRY about the consequence."

HOAGLAND: He thought of no particular consequence but "I had a quick thought that it was not going to end up well." . . . He had that transient thought.

FOX: And he said his contemplation ended when he heard a girl named Jackie say "I heard you changed your name" and he said "I changed it to Latisha" and he said he snapped and he shot her. You said "What was so disturbing about that name change?" and he said "It was so shocking and disgusting that he would do that."

HOAGLAND: Yes.

At the time of the shooting, Latisha was fifteen years old. Brandon had turned fourteen three weeks before. Some days prior Brandon had tried unsuccessfully to enlist friends to "jump" and "shank" her. This, he explained, was because he felt "disrespected" by an incident that had occurred in the hallway some days before. As chapter 1 will relate, it was alleged that during the encounter, Latisha said something to Brandon, something that ended with the word "baby." According to Brandon, it was the worst thing that anyone had ever said to him. This brief exchange in the hallway in between classes, according to Dr. Hoagland, was the "trigger incident" that set Brandon on the path to murder. And the name "Latisha" on a computer screen was, Brandon said, the final straw that led to the killing.

o o o

Brandon was charged with first-degree murder. He was also charged with a hate crime. The hate crime charge asserted that Larry King was killed because he was gay. The court and the testimony used the terms "gay" and sometimes "queer" to describe him, as did the children at school. But even as they used the name "Larry," to which Latisha answered, understood her to be a boy, and referred to her as gay, those categorical names referring to sexual orientation—"gay" and "queer"—very quickly gave way to descriptions of Larry's gender presentation.

ASSISTANT DISTRICT ATTORNEY MAEVE FOX: How well did you know Larry King?

CLASSMATE ABIAM M.: Honestly I didn't know him very well. I never spoke to him.

FOX: Is there a reason why you didn't speak to him or you just didn't?

ABIAM: Well, honestly just because of the fact that, you know, he was gay, I didn't really speak to him, so—

FOX: What was it about him that made you think he was gay?

ABIAM: Um, the way he dressed, you know, just stuff like that.

FOX: Anything about the way he acted?

ABIAM: No. Well, 'cause I wasn't really around him when he was, you know—I never was around him enough to know how he acted.

Abiam confirms here that he was not friends with Latisha because "he was gay." He marks his own frankness— "honestly," twice—in naming homosexuality as the reason he never spoke to Latisha. But what he describes is not any action of Latisha's; Abiam asserts that he was "never around him enough to know how he acted." "Larry" was "gay" because of the way "he" dressed. That is, like a girl:

Q: Do you know whether or not Larry King was at E. O. Green in sixth grade when you were in sixth grade?

A: Mmm, I don't remember.

Q: Do you know whether he was in seventh grade at E. O. Green when you were in seventh grade at E.O. Green?

A: I believe he was actually eighth grade.

Q: And then you know he was there in eighth grade.

A: Yeah.

Q: Did you observe any change in his manner of behavior or dress from the seventh grade through the eighth grade?

A: Yeah. In the eighth grade he was wearing women's clothing, like heels and stuff like that.

Q: What else?

A: That's really—really that's all I remember is just him wearing heels, and I never really paid attention to what else he wore.

Q: Okay. Did you ever see him wear a dress?

A: I don't remember him wearing a dress. I remember him wearing the little—the Playboy bunny on—as a necklace. I remember that.

Q: If you saw him wearing a dress, would that be something that you would probably remember?

A: Yeah.

Q: How about makeup or anything like that?

A: Makeup, yeah, he wore makeup.

Q: Eye makeup?

A: Yeah.

Q: Did you ever see in your—in the two years that you remember Larry King being at E. O. Green, did you ever see him doing anything physically aggressive to any other students?

A: No. All I seen was—all I saw was him chasing somebody.[3]

III. NOT WHY, BUT HOW

There are many ways to tell this story, and many stories inside of it. One might tell it as a story about school shootings and gun violence. Or about the criminal justice system. Or the systemic violences of class inequality. Or gentrification. Foster care. Transracial adoption. Adolescent prosecution. Hate crimes law. White supremacy. Adolescent psychology. My colleague and friend Dr. Ken Corbett, whom I sat next to in the courtroom for the duration of the murder trial, describes many of these aspects of the case in his book *A Murder over a Girl*, for which he interviewed dozens of the people involved. If you are interested in this story, and understanding the lives of the people involved in it, his book is essential reading.

The question that was asked after this killing, perhaps after any killing, by the people involved was: Why? Why did Brandon shoot his classmate? There could be many answers to that question. "Why" is not quite the question I will be trying to ask or answer in this book. What I will be asking in *The Life and Death of Latisha King* is *how*? Not the how of the murder; those facts are not in dispute. Brandon McInerney brought a gun to school, concealed in the pocket of his sweatshirt. He took a seat behind Latisha King and sat there quietly for twenty minutes, then he stood up and fired two shots into the back of Latisha's head. The question of "how" becomes a question of what created the conditions of possibility for that shooting. I will be asking how that question of "why" is taken up and followed in the case and, in particular, how Latisha's gender was understood in the context of the school, in the courtroom, and how the events in the courtroom framed the events of the shooting.

My book investigates how gender operated in this case. I will analyze how gender is read as a provocation, how the legal proceedings justified the act of murderous violence directed at Latisha King as defensive based on a reading of her gender as itself constituting an act, and an aggressive one. Queer or trans gender becomes a target of homophobic and transphobic aggression through first being read as itself constituting an act of aggression. I also want to read the modes of argumentation through which this recasting of violence came about, the ways in which the expressiveness of the bodies of the teachers and the lawyers and the witnesses step in to take over the function of argumentation in those moments during the trial where language finds its limit. I claim that these bodily modes of expression that asserted themselves in the courtroom paradoxically became a visible supplement that was invisible to the official transcript and the legal record.

The first half of the book addresses these questions by turning to phenomenological analyses of walking, since walking played a surprisingly central role in the case. In chapters 1 and 2 I will read the ways in which Latisha King's walk was described and read. But I will also concentrate on the bodily movements of the participants of the trial. In this way, I want to proceed by way of a kind of methodological reversal. Whereas in the trial Latisha's body and bodily movements were subject to the greatest scrutiny, I attempt here to turn that gaze toward the gazers themselves, to take up the resources of phenomenology in order to subject the bodily movements of the onlookers to the same degree of scrutiny that Latisha received during the testimony.

In chapter 1, "Comportment" I take up the notion of bodily orientation. There I suggest that phenomenological description can help elucidate the embodied performance of non-normative genders such as Latisha's, and the transphobic and homophobic reactions to such gender performances evident in the trial. The shooting took place after a long campaign of harassment centered on her gender presentation and perceived sexual orientation, in which Latisha's classmates bullied her for dressing, sounding, and walking "like a fag" and "like a girl." The defense attorneys in the subsequent murder trial attempted to rebut the accusation of bullying by suggesting that Latisha was the perpetrator rather than the victim of harassment. McInerney's lawyers claimed that it was Latisha's inappropriately gendered movement, her walking "like a girl," that constituted harassment of those around her. Drawing on Erwin Straus's "The Upright Posture," most familiar today as the foil against which Iris Marion Young launched her trenchant critique of phenomenology's gender biases in "Throwing like a Girl," I argue that a phenomenology of walking illuminates the ways in which Latisha's gender was read in the classroom. The chapter concludes by turning to phenomenological description to unpack the performance of gender in the courtroom itself, exploring how queer gender was mimetically enacted in and through the bodies of the attorneys during the trial and how the courtroom emerged as a second site of gender panic.

In chapter 2, "Movement," I lean into the phenomenological concept of motricity, or movement, to think about the ways in which bodily movement and sound worked in this case. Using Maurice Merleau-Ponty's theorizations of gesture, style, and bodily movement in his essay "Indirect Language and the Voices of Silence," I read witness descriptions of Latisha King, and also read the bodily movements of the lawyers, the witnesses, and the spectators in the courtroom during the trial. Merleau-Ponty's theorization of bodily movement as disclosive of gendered meaning helps us to interpret Latisha's walk and to understand the different ways in which gendered meaning was ascribed to that walk and to her. In this section of the book, I also examine the ways that bodily movement was expressive of meaning inside the courtroom itself. During the trial, in moments when the language around gender and sexuality became difficult or unspeakable, when language started to fail, embodied and wordless movement took over the expressive function of the spoken word. At several points when the testimony started to veer into uncomfortable territory and discussion of Latisha's sexuality threatened to be explicit, the lawyers would shift registers and begin to advance their arguments in a way no written transcript could capture. By citationally acting out "queerness" with their own bodies, they summoned the dead Latisha King into the courtroom through mimetically acting out a parody of her imagined gestures and her walking. These episodes of pantomime and charade during the testimony show the ways in which gender and sexuality, despite their ubiquity, were often unspeakable during the trial.

Chapter 2 concludes by reading Latisha's racial identity, and the performance and erasure of race in the case, by turning to another King case, the beating of black motorist Rodney King in 1991, to explore how attributions of aggression worked there and exemplified the ways in which violence becomes projected onto vulnerable subjects in order to justify the violence used against them as defensive, rather than punitive or retaliatory. The first part of the book ends with a coda reading another final turn of aggression, considering the suicides of queer and trans youth alongside Freud's assessment of suicide as a "murder of the self."

The second half of the book also reads the body, but the body understood more broadly, inclusive of the social body of the school in which the murder happened and of the bodies of objects used as physical evidence during the trial. In chapter 3, "Anonymity," I turn to the concept of anonymity in the work of phenomenologists Merleau-Ponty and Alfred Schütz and consider the role anonymity plays in several areas of phenomenological inquiry: otherness, common sense, and the social world. The concept of anonymity offers a helpful way to mediate between phenomenology understood as a transcendental project or an "eidetic science" in Husserl's words and phenomenology as the study of the perspectival situatedness of, and local practices in, the social world. Recent feminist phenomenology has turned to anonymity in order to think about the function of gender in the social world, and I will suggest that anonymity understood in this sense can help elucidate the events surrounding the murder. Specifically, I argue that Latisha was denied this form of anonymity, an anonymity that comprises the tissue which holds us into daily and mundane being-in-the-world with others, and that this denial had an effect that was both particularizing and dehumanizing.

The first three chapters explore the ways in which gender in this case was a gestural phenomenon. In the book's final chapter, I look at those moments in the trial in which gender was conferred by objects and describe the ways in which gender functioned as what Merleau-Ponty calls an "ultra-chose," a thing that can be observed but never fully comprehended. In both cases—gender as gesture and gender as object—gender is understood as something other than a property of bodies or persons. I will take up some of the objects that in Latisha's life and in the murder trial came to mark and signify gender. In these moments when the gaze of the courtroom was focused on objects, not just described but brought out and physically handled in the courtroom, the defense lawyers were attempting to turn gender from an effect of gesture into a property of objects. I also try to think a bit about the ways in which gender itself became consolidated as an object during this trial, as neither an effect of gestures nor a property of objects, but a thing in its own right, and a dangerous thing. Gender, I will argue, became weaponized.

Finally, I consider how responsibility was invoked in the aftermath of the trial. How is responsibility invoked when we talk about violence of this kind? During the trial, one teacher recalled her pronouncement that "if something wasn't done soon," there would be trouble with Larry. The ambiguity of that phrase, I claim, eloquently telegraphed the teacher's own homophobia, her insistence that in order to protect Larry King from the threat of violence that was rising invisibly but palpably toward him, he needed to be protected not from Brandon McInerney, but from his own gender expression, from himself, from Latisha.

IV. CRITICAL PHENOMENOLOGY

For the matter of method, the how of dealing with the how, I draw on phenomenology to analyze each of these aspects of the case.[4] Phenomenology is a philosophical tradition concerned with how the world gives itself to appearances, and the structures of consciousness through which we apprehend that givenness. It has its origins in the work of philosopher Edmund Husserl and developed through the twentieth century, particularly in France and Germany. "Phenomenology" does not name a unified school of thought, but designates a diverse number of thinkers in philosophy and the social sciences concerned with perception, the relation between human existence and meaning, and what Husserl named the "lifeworld" and its structures. Common to all phenomenology is careful attention to how the world is delivered to us through our perceptions. Phenomenology is also a method, committed to perpetual beginning as a way of apprehending the world and our place in it. Phenomenologists note the ways in which habit and familiarity shape our understandings of what is real and true; phenomenological methods endeavor to approach our surroundings anew, shedding our sedimented interpretations so that we might apprehend the world and the things in it with greater clarity. Since it takes as its central concern how things appear in the world, phenomenology is particularly useful for understanding the Latisha King case in that it offers a way to understand the meanings that accrue around bodily movement. Phenomenology is uniquely valuable because it proceeds by attending, in a thorough and detailed way, to perception, to what and how we perceive.

First-person experience is the zero-point of phenomenology, to which it constantly and repeatedly returns. Its aim is to render explicit, through careful description, what had heretofore been implicit. Yet for many phenomenologists, the result of phenomenology's methodological reliance on first-person experience is not necessarily fortification of personhood, not the shoring-up of a sovereign subject. Despite its first-person vantage point, this phenomenology is advocating neither subjectivism nor solipsism. There is no perception without a subject, but there is no subject without a world. A subject only becomes so through her enmeshment within a world, and for phenomenologists such as Merleau-Ponty and Emmanuel Levinas, the project of phenomenology is an elucidation of the ties between self and world, an illumination of the mutual and necessary enmeshment of the two. For phenomenologists such as these, our world is always an intersubjective one, lived through *Mitsubjectivität*, to use Husserl's word. As Merleau-Ponty puts it in "In Praise of Philosophy": "Our relationship to the true passes through others. Either we go towards the true with them, or it is not towards the true that we are going."[5]

Recent work in phenomenology has focused on the intersubjective nature of the world and the relations of power through which that intersubjectivity forms, and much of this work has engaged issues of social justice, of racial inequality, of gender and sexuality, of incarceration. Lisa Guenther has termed this "critical phenomenology." In her book *Solitary Confinement: Social Death and Its Afterlives*, Guenther examines incarceration and punishment using critical phenomenology, which she defines this way:

> By critical phenomenology I mean a method that is rooted in first-person accounts of experience but also critical of classical phenomenology's claim that the first person singular is absolutely prior to intersubjectivity and to the complex textures of social life. The critical edge of this approach emerges through an engagement with the work of Frantz Fanon, Maurice Merleau-Ponty, and Emmanuel Levinas. . . . I have sought to develop a method of critical phenomenology that both continues the phenomenological tradition of taking first-person experience as the starting point for philosophical reflection and also resists the tendency of phenomenologists to privilege transcendental *subjectivity* over transcendental *intersubjectivity*.[6]

We will revisit this tension in phenomenology between the personal and the transcendental in the chapters that follow. Critical phenomenology may answer to that name, or it may go by others. It might depart from classical phenomenology, or it might locate itself squarely inside phenomenology's most traditional forms.[7] For some phenomenologists, "phenomenology *is* critical philosophy."[8]

Phenomenology, then, involves a particular way of describing what is, a way of mapping the terrain of what appears. In phenomenological inquiry, when we expose the dualisms of self and other, of subject and object, to the light of experience, the separation between them begins to dissolve. When we are able to suspend our traditional modes of philosophical thinking and allow ourselves to encounter situations, objects, and other people with perceptual openness, we lose ourselves in them, a losing that unravels our bounded sense of ourselves and illuminates our enmeshment with other things and other beings. Phenomenology is an invitation to awaken anew to the world, and in this it opens onto an ethics of perception and coexistence, as we shall see in chapter 4.

In the course of everyday life, we take the world as it is; we do not conjure and project another world beneath or behind the world as it appears. But when we submit our experiences of our daily life to reflection, we can see that this world is built up over time. We can understand that it is constituted by and appears as a result of certain conditions. We understand that the aspect of itself that the world presents to us is necessarily partial and incomplete, and dependent on our own orientation. And when our own orientation is something other than straight, the world that we inhabit is also different. Its horizons might be altered. Indeed, that experience of having one's horizons altered, of disorientation, is one of the queer things about phenomenology, as well as a hallmark of what Sara Ahmed has called "queer phenomenology." In her book by that name, she notes that in being oriented toward objects that are not heterosexual, and living through lines of kinship that are not straight, queer desire bring objects and others near to itself in ways "that might not have otherwise been reachable within the body horizon of the social."[9]

V. RACE UNDER ERASURE

If gender and sexuality were difficult to speak about in the courtroom, race was literally disallowed. The hate crime charge asserted that Latisha King was killed because she was gay. It was determined in a pretrial hearing that race played no part in the killing and therefore would not be part of trial. This is a parsing that is legally possible but phenomenologically nonsensical: neither the experience nor the perception of gender can be divorced from race. It was hatred that took the form of homophobia, rather than hatred stemming from racism, that was central during the trial, even though Brandon McInerney was white and Latisha King was biracial and identified as black. Several days of testimony were given over to proving that Brandon McInerney was a budding white supremacist, even as the prosecution was not able to argue that racial hatred was a motivating factor in the case. That is, the testimony about race in the courtroom centered on Brandon McInerney's whiteness, not Latisha King's blackness. In the parts of the transcript analyzed in this book, discussion of Latisha's race is absent, as it was for almost all of the testimony about Brandon's relationship to Latisha. This rendering invisible of the racial identity of the victim of violent hatred was, to use Toni Morrison's words, an "act of enforcing racelessness," which, she reminds us, "is itself a racial act."[10]

During the trial, the presence of race and racial anxiety could often be read even through that absence; descriptions of Latisha as "aggressive" demonstrate a phobic relation to race as well as, and as intertwined with, gender and sexuality, an anxiety that Wallace Best has termed "the fear of black bodies in motion."[11] Latisha was characterized as disruptive, as unruly. As Falguni Sheth teaches us, the unruly is a racialized category that can serve as a "lightening rod" to consolidate and alienate certain populations, to mark them as strange, as dangerous. She notes "the transformation of the unfamiliar into a sense of wrongdoing on the part of the 'strange' group itself—in modern parlance, a 'blaming of the victim,' so to speak."[12]

o o o

Latisha's life, and her death, comes into clearer focus when read in the context of the lives, and the disproportional rates of death, of trans women of color in this country. We can recall the case of Tyra Hunter, who died after being refused medical treatment after a car accident in 1995 after first responders discovered that she was trans. Or Gwen Araujo, another trans teen of color murdered in Southern California in 2002. As C. Riley Snorton and Jin Haritaworn remind us in their discussion of the Tyra Hunter case in their essay "Trans Necropolitics," "It is necessary to think specifically of transgender of color experiences as distinct from queer subjectivities."[13] Or as Latisha's classmate Aliyah put it in the film *Valentine Road*: "I don't think Larry is gay. He's transgendered. It's a big difference." It is essential to ask: How do such misattributions happen, both in real-time and in the quite unreal-time of the courtroom? As we do this thinking, as we #SayTheirNames, we need to attend to the uniquely precarious social positioning of trans-of-color lives, and at the same time resist the cultural impulse to ascribe fatality to these lives, to collect all trans-of-color lives under the sign of death.[14]

> ASSISTANT DISTRICT ATTORNEY MAEVE FOX: At some point did Larry make a request of you that you call him by a certain name?
>
> DAWN BOLDRIN: He did.
>
> FOX: Do you remember that?
>
> BOLDRIN: I do.
>
> FOX: What did he ask you to—what did he want to be called?
>
> BOLDRIN: Um, I believe it was Latisha.
>
> FOX: What did you tell him in response to that?
>
> BOLDRIN: Told him no. He would have to officially have his name changed before I'd do that.

In 2004, two years after Gwen Arajuo's murder, her mother petitioned the court to posthumously change her name, legally, from her male given name to Gwen Amber Rose Araujo. The petition was granted. Two years later, Gwen's name entered into the law a second time, in the form of California Assembly Bill 1160, the "Gwen Araujo Justice for Victims Act." This 2006 bill outlawed the use of either "gay panic" or "trans panic" defenses in criminal murder trials in the state of California. Five years later, defense attorneys Scott Wippert and Robyn Bramson used a "gay panic" strategy in their defense of Brandon MacInerney in the killing of Larry King despite such strategies being disallowed in California by the Gwen Araujo Act.

Larry King's friend Averi reported that Larry had tried out a few different names for what she called his "alter-egos" and had this to say about the genesis of her name.

"Everyone knew that Larry was part black. So it was like a generic kind of black name. You don't mess with Latoya or Latonya. You don't mess with her." And Latisha, the variant she finally settled on, was not to be messed with either. Her coming out, her announcement of this name, was as much a racial as a gendered coming out, a claiming of a racial identity that was visible, if rarely named. Latisha, a black trans girl, was never named as such, was instead always named in court as Larry, a gay boy whose race was not speakable. Latisha's name, like her life, was short-lived.

VI. A NOTE ON NAMES AND PRONOUNS

I have said that phenomenology proceeds by way of description, by taking careful account of what appears. One might ask: How can this be a phenomenology, when I never observed Latisha King? She only ever appeared in the courtroom in fragments, pathologized, misgendered, deracialized. My reading of Latisha's gender as "girl" flies in the face of the official record. And my attention to her race is read for the most part through its legal omissions. The courtroom gave us a picture of Larry King, not Latisha King. Even in those moments when she did emerge in court, ghostly, conjured through photographs or descriptions or objects, there was much space and time between those images and Latisha as a living, breathing girl. How can one offer a phenomenology of what does not appear? I would respond that phenomenology does indeed insist that we read what appears, but this need not be reduced to positivism, or to restrict our thinking to only the realm of what is manifest. What appears is always conditioned and made possible by that which does not. The real is always circumscribed and realized through the imagined.

It is sometimes only through the work of imagining that we can hope to contest the hegemony of racist and transphobic logics and illogics. So my readings of Latisha, and in particular the ways in which she was gendered and racialized, are readings of absence as well as presence, imaginings that try to animate what is occluded and its relationship to what is manifest. Our reality cannot be disentangled from the racist and transphobic imaginaries that underlie it, and the work of resisting such imaginaries rely on that same work of imagining. In the words of David Marriott: "We can contest the dreamwork of racist culture in its verisimilitude, address and imagine another kind of *experience*, another kind of living present and future."[15]

I have called her "Latisha," because that is what she called herself. And that is what she asked several of her friends, her teachers, and the people at the youth shelter where she lived to call her. That she chose this name, and requested to be called by it at school and other places, is more significant to me than the fact that few were willing to comply. That many of them refused to do so does not, to my mind, alter the truth that "Latisha" was how she understood herself and wanted to be understood by others. I am also referring to her as transgender, which, if we follow Susan Stryker's definition of that term in *Transgender History* as naming "any and all kinds of variation from gender norms and expectations" is incontrovertibly accurate.[16]

Nevertheless, there will be some inconsistency in my use of gendered names and pronouns throughout this book. As I argue, this story was misrepresented in the press as a gay story when it should more properly understood as a trans one, as many trans stories historically have been. In this way, the trans narrative is covered and effaced by a narrative of homosexuality, a narrative that gained traction and proliferated in media coverage and legal prosecution of her death. In talking about Latisha and using feminine pronouns to describe her, I am hoping to reflect and retain the bid for a feminine identity that she was making by claiming the name Latisha, and I will also use feminine pronouns in order to represent this. But it is also important to see the effects that resulted when institutions, the school that policed her gender, and the court that adjudicated the killing, understood Larry King to be only a boy. In those places where I refer to Larry by that name or with male pronouns, my intention is to reflect most accuracy how the court and school described "him" and to illuminate with clarity the homophobic and transphobic logics that dictated the ways in which "he" was treated. Representing the ways in which this social identity was seen, and sometimes lived, as "boy" is the only way to make clear the injustices that happened in the media, in the school, and in the court; conversely, using the female pronoun exclusively to refer to her would "correct the record" in a way that would obscure the injustice that Latisha received. So in those instances where I do use the male pronoun, I am attempting to describe with most precision exactly how Latisha's gender was read and misread, and I have done my best to do this describing without replicating the violences done to her in the name of gender conformity.

Latisha's declaration of her name and self-definition as a girl were not incidental to the killing. That declaration was, I will hope to show, the moment that sparked it. And her name lived on the computer screen for only a flickering few minutes before Brandon McInerney assured that the name, and the girl who wore it, would disappear.

1

COMPORTMENT

I've always been obsessed with high heels but as a child I was not allowed to have them. Oftentimes I would sashay around on tip toes imagining that I had high heels on and I was constantly looking over my shoulders to make sure I didn't get caught or that I wasn't being judged. Let's face it, when you're a transchild you've got to watch your ass.

—Justin Vivian Bond, *Tango: My Childhood, Backwards and in High Heels*

I. DRESSING, TELLING, PASSING

In 2008, Latisha King was shot to death at E. O. Green Junior High School by her classmate Brandon McInerney. It was the first class of the day, Dawn Boldrin's English comp class. Latisha was seated at a computer, and Brandon was seated behind her. Twenty minutes into class, Brandon stood up, pulled a gun from the pocket of his sweatshirt, and fired one bullet into Latisha's head. Latisha slumped down in her seat, bleeding profusely. Ms. Boldrin screamed: "What the fuck are you doing, Brandon?!" Brandon paused and made eye contact with Ms. Boldrin before firing a second shot into the back of Latisha's head.

o o o

After the shooting, before the murder trial, the local newspaper, the *Ventura County Star*, ran scores of articles about the murder, its prosecution in the courts, and the family backgrounds of the victim and the shooter. The victim was referred to by male pronouns and the name "Larry King" exclusively. Scant mention was made of the name "Lati-sha." And nearly every story written in the paper contained this sentence: *King, an eighth-grader, dressed in a feminine manner and told friends that he was gay.*[1] What exactly is being conveyed to the readers of the *Ventura County Star* through the repeated refrain of this sentence? To claim that someone dresses "in a feminine manner" is not a nonsensical claim, although it is vague, demonstrating, or perhaps generating, a lack of clarity as to what precisely is being modified by that term "feminine." That vagueness attends the reading of Latisha's dress—just what is a "man-ner" of dressing, and what counts as a "feminine" manner, exactly? Is it the clothing that is feminine, or the way that King dons and carries that clothing? Assertions about the manner of her dressing figure us in a spectatorial relation to King, privy to the privacy of her room and the particu-larity of her body, even as the pronouncement about that manner of dressing—feminine—throws us back into the public realm, the social context in which such distinctions between masculine and feminine in clothing and behavior are parsed and judged.

In 2009 the *Ventura County Star* published almost the same sentence, with the phrase "dressed in a feminine manner" morphing to the less vague but still more odd "wore female clothing": "King wore female clothing and told classmates he was gay."[2] This locution asserts the dressing as a matter of sex rather than gender, and offers the object of that sexing as the clothing itself, rather than its wearer. In this logic, instead of clothing conferring a gender on us, it is we who must match the sex of our clothing. Even if we understand "female" to refer to the proper wearer of the clothing, there is still some attribu-

tional sleight-of-hand in describing "Larry King's" clothing as female; the clothing bears the sex of persons not
wearing it. In 2010, the *Ventura County Star* appeared to
settle on the phrase "feminine attire": "King, 15, dressed in
feminine attire and told friends he was gay."[3] Here swapping out "attire" for "clothing" seems to make the materiality of what is worn still less concrete, and also to shift, ever
so slightly, the class signification of the outfit.

These are small differences, not without significance,
though perhaps minor in media we know to be all-too-
normative. Nonetheless, each of these statements understands itself to be asserting, fundamentally, the same
claim—a claim, however, that is not entirely clear about
either Larry King's gender or his sexuality. When it is asserted that Larry wore female clothing and told friends he
was gay, is that "and" inclusive or disjunctive? If the former, then in offering two modes of action—dressing and
speaking—the sentence is describing two manifestations
of the same phenomenon. Larry was queer, and queerness comes out in all sorts of ways, speaking and dressing
among them. If that "and" is disjunctive, however, then
the sentence does not offer Larry as a queer subject who
lives his queerness in various modes but rather offers him
as a queer subject through his telling ("told friends he was
gay") and a trans subject in his mode of bodily presentation ("dressed in feminine attire"). The telling and the
dressing are two different modes of expression that an-
nounce two different kinds of identification, the first of
gender and the second of sexuality. The assertion would
be that there are two poles of transgression here, dressing
in feminine attire on the one hand and gay self-disclosure
on the other, and the *Ventura County Star* is offering each
as separate but equally provocative. Gender is expressed

by clothing, or in this case, an external perception of that clothing's proper gender. Sexuality, in this case, is expressed not through behavior but through disclosure, or through disclosure as behavior.

In each case, Latisha's dressing and her telling, her gender and her sexuality are almost entirely removed from the bodily realm. As an epistemological claim, "Larry told friends he was gay" asserts that Larry's gayness both consists of and is revealed by his own utterance. That utterance then reenters the public realm of the *Ventura County Star* through circuitous travels through "friends," which figures the proper domain of queer self-disclosure as the private realm, and by implication circulating more widely only though gossip, hearsay, or rumor. The framing of this disclosure places us already in the realms of the feminine and of that which is shameful. According to newspaper reports, the direct object of Larry's self-disclosure shifts from 2008 to 2009. Whereas the earlier sentence has King telling friends he was gay, the sentence from 2009 asserts that he "told classmates he was gay." The last seems to offer a hysterical subject, inappropriately disclosing all over the place, provocatively disseminating his sexuality throughout the classroom and the school. It appears, however, that Larry's "gay behavior" consisted entirely of disclosing to a few people that he was gay; it is not clear that his "gay behavior" was anything *other* than the speech act of that disclosure. In other words, it may be that the declaration of gayness was itself the only queer behavior that he engaged in, as is sometimes true for queer youth. It is worth noting that Latisha had gone to another school before E. O. Green and that she changed schools because she had been harassed for being gay for well over a year at the prior school. It is a particular irony that the "gay lifestyle," in this case, refers almost exclusively to being bullied and tormented by other students, chased from school to school, and rejected at home, rather than actually naming any variety of sexual expression.

The national media attention the story received in the weeks and months and years after the shooting for the most part followed the local press and read Larry King as a gay teenager rather than a trans teenager, but also retained attention to Larry's transgressive gender expression. In this it would appear that the media wants to have its trans spectacle and its gay identity both, and in asserting them simultaneously in the same sentence these articles seem, in a rather transparent act of projection, to diagnose the confusion as Larry's. It seems that the logic at work in this kind of reportage is an instance of trans erasure, that what we are seeing when "Larry" is described as "gay" is the all-too-familiar subsuming of a trans identity into a more easily assimilable gay identity—a distressingly common way of both denying and appropriating the trans community, which differentially bears violence that the more easily assimilated do not.

Sexual identity and gender identity are lived simultaneously, are mutually constituting, are wrapped thoroughly around one another. Why, then, belabor the parsing of gender and sexual identity in this instance, if the two always accompany one another and are so thoroughly imbricated? I want to suggest that homophobic and transphobic conflations of gender expression and sexual identity can have a very specific and real effect. Consider, for example, the characterization of Latisha's gender expression offered by one of the administrators at E. O. Green Junior High, who stated that "we have a student expressing his sexuality through makeup." At one level it is a simple muddle, a swapping out of gender for sexuality: what the administrator labels "sexual expression" should more accurately be described as "gender expression." The implication of this simple swap, though, turns out to be not so simple. Conceiving of gender expression and sexual identity as fungible encourages people to look at gender expression as an act, and often *as an aggressive act*, akin to a sexual advance or even a sexual assault. This may be one way of understanding the otherwise mystifyingly disproportionate response to non-normative gender expression. Readings of Latisha's gender presentation imply that her assertion of identity was a social event, asking something of others in asserting something about herself. Whereas normative gender identity, in this logic, asks nothing and demands nothing of others—it is, in effect, non-social—trans gender is understood as a provocation to the extent that is a shared social project. Some of the legal maneuvers related to the case would later reflect this logic: in suggesting that Latisha's gender expression provoked Brandon McInerney to violence, they suggested in essence that by expressing her gender identity, Latisha authored her own murder.

II. IN FULL SWING

The shooting took place after a long campaign of harassment targeting Latisha's gender presentation and perceived sexual orientation, in which her classmates bullied her for dressing, sounding, and walking "like a fag" and "like a girl." The defense in the murder trial attempted to rebut the accusations of bullying by suggesting that Latisha was the perpetrator, rather than the victim, of bullying and harassment. Brandon McInerney and his lawyers claimed that "Larry's" dressing, sounding, and walking "like a girl" constituted harassment of those around him. Here we see one of the dangers of conflating gender identity and sexual identity; in this case, gender presentation becomes interpreted as a form of sexual behavior, and that "behavior" is marked and read as aggressive in order to legitimate the violence that is visited upon the gender-transgressive person, violence with disciplinary and normativizing aims. The legal defense proceeded by way of reversal, a turning back against the trans child, so that the one who was murdered became the one who was judged and found guilty of aggression.

Latisha's femininity made her stand out. In the seventh grade, when Larry still seemed to his classmates and teachers to be a boy, though perhaps a feminine one, few people could recall who he was. Later, however, he was seen as overwhelmingly, distressingly feminine. The heightening of Latisha's femininity was read and described throughout the murder trial as a "turning point" in her behavior. We might pause to consider that turning. Gender here is understood as behavior, and as a volitional behavior, a matter of choosing, willing, deciding. Indeed, Dr. Donald Hoagland, the psychologist called as an expert witness by the defense team during the trial, asserted that Larry's behavior, by which he meant Latisha's femininity, was difficult for the other children to deal with and made them uncomfortable. This discomfort, he explained, arose because at that point in adolescence the students are coming to a sense of their own sexuality. The heteronormative scope of the developmental narrative invoked by Dr. Hoagland was not understood to include Latisha; rather, it pertained only to the presumptively heterosexual boys and girls whom she might have "confused" through her "behavior." In contrast, then, with the cisgendered boys and girls against whom she was compared, Latisha's gender was seen as a choice, as a behavior over which she had control, and also construed as something over which she refused to exert control. Latisha's gender was characterized simultaneously as the product of her will and as the result of her failure to exert that will. An additional difficulty with this characterization was its failure to recognize that Latisha was coming into a surer and firmer sense of her gender as she approached adolescence. Just as the rest of the boys were, just as the rest of the girls were.

One of the primary ways that Latisha's gender was read was through her way of walking. Walk and gender are both real and materially expressed, though neither can be reduced to the materiality that does the expressing. Gender and walk are situated between material body and immaterial inhabitation of the body. The walk resides in the hinge between the volitional (where my feet take me) and the nonvolitional (my walk as unintentionally disclosing my gender or sexuality). The walk has a style that changes over time as it develops, even as its temporal dislocation points backward. Walking is an act that we perform with our habit-body. We build up this habit-body over time, slowly, starting with our first few toddling steps. The style that any walk will eventually develop is unavoidably inflected with gendered meanings, as well as racial and class markers, which strengthen and deepen and become more pronounced in adolescence, developing like other characteristics of gender. That Latisha's walk was read as a manifestation of her gender, and as evidence of her improper inhabitation of gender, was demonstrated by Dawn Boldrin, the teacher in whose classroom the shooting occurred. When asked about Larry and what made him stand out from the other children, she suggests that it was something about gender. The queerness of Larry's gender was visible yet not easy to describe, and Boldrin ends up locating gender in Larry's gestures. She is asked during the trial about the first time that she met Larry, the year before the shooting. "In terms of masculinity or femininity," asks prosecutor Maeve Fox, "where you would you put him on the scale?" "He was obviously feminine," Boldrin responds. "How so?" asks Fox. "Um . . ."[4]

Boldrin pauses. At that time, when Larry was in seventh grade, she perceived him to be feminine in a way that was easy to see but difficult to locate. This was before the cross-gender accessories that Latisha donned in the ten days before her death—makeup, earrings, high-heeled boots—the "behavior" that would attract so much attention, and so much anger, in her eighth-grade year. Struggling to articulate this attribute of Larry's that was at once so discernible and so diffuse, so bodily and so not-quite-material, she offers: "I guess his size, his petiteness, by the way, his mannerisms, the way he carried himself, he had more of the qualities of a girl than a boy. Especially at that age, it's pretty distinct the boys versus the girls at that age." There is a distinct difference between the comportment of the boys and the comportment of the girls, says Boldrin, and Larry falls on the girls' side of that line. But the "versus" in that "boys vs girls" does more work than just indicating difference. "Boys vs girls" is a distinction that is oppositional and incompossible. Latisha's girlishness is attributable to some things over which she has no control—"his size, his petiteness"—and other things that she is thought to be able to control, "his mannerisms, the way he carried himself." Referring to this girlishness, Maeve Fox asks, "Did that seem apparent to the other students?" Boldrin responds: "Oh yes. I don't think he was throwing it at people, but it was more his personality. You walk down the street and you see two men, I think you can distinguish which one is masculine and which one is feminine and that's just the way it is."

Gender is figured as a potential projectile, something that Latisha could be "throwing at people," but did not, at least not in the seventh grade. Ms. Boldrin seems to suggest that gender-as-thrown describes gender as the province of the surface, of bodily appearance, of material aspects of the body that are more concrete than a walk or comportment. Those last are understood to be something more akin to "personality," to a way that one inhabits the body, an individuated style. Throwing it at people, she intimates, is what happened later, with the makeup, the earrings, and the boots. Boldrin here offers a reformulation of Freud's assertion that the first thing you notice about someone walking down the street is whether that person is a man or a woman. Freud conjures a solitary figure walking down the street, surrounded by people who discern and judge, singly and collectively forming an audience for his or her gender expression. In place of this solitary figure Boldrin offers a pair, a couple, walking down the street, but rather than a heterosexual pairing of a man and a woman in which we would immediately know which was which, Boldrin substitutes a feminine man for the woman. With that swap, the pairing of masculinity with femininity is retained, as is the insistence that we all know the difference. The insistence is that we can all spot the girly boy, and immediately, and from twenty paces. We can tell that the girly boy does not quite pass for a boy, even in passing. Latisha's gender was read not only off of her body, but also from how her body expressed itself, how she carried that body through the school. Boldrin described Latisha's gender in eighth grade as being "in full swing," using a figure of speech that seems to refer to the femininity of the walk, that swing of the hip that constitutes a swish, as much as anything else.[5]

∘ ∘ ∘

On the morning of the shooting, Dawn Boldrin pulled Latisha aside at the beginning of class to talk with her about her academic progress. The class had a paper due that day, and Latisha had chosen protest songs of the 1960s as her topic, but her paper was not finished, perhaps not even started. Latisha, never a good student, was doing quite poorly this term, failing several classes, and was in danger of failing the eighth grade. She told Latisha "that eighth-grade graduation was coming up and if he wanted to actually walk he would need to really start focusing on his academics."[6] Here, "walk" is a metonym for graduation, where the student's walk under a proscenium and across a stage signifies and performs the completion of her passage through some portion of her schooling and her transition, in this case, to high school. The content of the conditional involves Latisha's desire—"*if* he wanted to walk"—but its form intimates the likelihood of her failure. Boldrin suggests that the accomplishment of the walk is uncertain, and that Latisha's relation to the possibility of successfully walking is one of desire rather than probability. If she wanted to walk properly, if she wanted her walk to count as a walk at all, certain conditions would have to be met, conditions that Latisha had failed to meet in the past, conditions that, Boldrin was concerned, she would continue to fail to meet. Since she kept failing, would continue to fail, at schoolwork, this other walk that signified in excess of itself was weighted more than other walks, was also something that she would fail, another walk that she would not be able to accomplish properly.

The defense attorneys argued that Latisha was harassing Brandon and that the shooting was thus a defensive rather than an aggressive act, an attempt to stop the harassment. This argument relied on the assumption that Latisha's walk came not only to signify but actually to enact Latisha's sexuality. The most surprising thing about the assertion of harassment is that the behavior characterized as harassment, in at least two instances, was exactly and only the walk itself. One incident the defense documented as an instance of Latisha harassing Brandon was Latisha's walking past a group of boys sitting on a bench. It sounds laughably innocuous thus described: How could simply walking past a group of people constitute harassment? As the defense attorneys and their expert psychologist took pains to show, it was the *way* Latisha walked that was so provocative. Boys report that they are uncomfortable around Latisha, uncomfortable when she sits down at their lunch table, uncomfortable when she walks by. The defense explains that sexual harassment is behavior that makes other people feel uncomfortable. Ergo: Latisha was sexually harassing the boys in the school, because her sexual (read: gender) behavior made people uncomfortable. The conclusion is made possible by reading gender behavior as sexual behavior. When a "queer" style of walking becomes the target of aggression, that targeting legitimates itself by projecting aggression into the walk, and thus onto the person walking. The queer walk is treated as if it were aggression itself. One (uncorroborated) version of the story reported that Latisha walked past the boys sitting on the bench, then paused to apply lip gloss. In that moment, behavior that is transgressing gender—that boy is putting on lip gloss!—is understood as harassment, as targeting the boys who are looking on. In the absence of any understanding that there could be such a thing as a boy who wears lip gloss, or, indeed, that Latisha might have been more of a girl than a boy, she was read as a boy who was choosing deliberate actions to make other boys uncomfortable. They called her "faggot" and ran away from her, or called her "faggot" and flattened themselves against their lockers to give her a ten-foot berth when she walked down the hallway, or called her "faggot" and left the lunch table when she sat down. The epithet was so commonplace that it did not register to the teachers as harassment. It was not unusual, it was every hour of every day, that Latisha was called a "fag." Ken Corbett has noted that as an epithet, "Faggot operates as a projectile," one with injurious force.[7] It is a word that expresses the "general boyhood quest to be big and winning, not small and losing," as Corbett makes clear.[8] The word was directed at Latisha with full awareness of its injurious capacity, at the same time as it was deployed with an almost casual contempt. It was not the word they were uncomfortable with, it was Latisha. Especially Brandon.

III. PASSING: AGE AND RACE

The homophobic hatred that was on display in descriptions of Latisha's interactions at school is both noteworthy and mundane, distressing and all too common. On the one hand, it was dismissed as just one of the ways that adolescents treat each other in junior high; the hatred was marked as casual and dismissed with remarks like "boys will be boys," in which that "will" is both descriptive and predictive, extrapolating from the ways in which boys treat each other in the present to advance an assertion about how they will no doubt treat each other, and treat otherly-gendered others, in the future. When the phrase is used to justify aggression, it points to contempt and hatred and aggression as the proper province of adolescent male behavior. In that phrase, "boys will be boys," the word "boys" in its first deployment names a gendered subject position and in its second a behavioral disposition. Thus boys (young men) will be boys (aggressors), reflexively, with the subject position necessarily congruent to disposition. Boys being boys will insure that they not be girls. "Boys" also names a developmental stage. Brandon shot Latisha three weeks after his fourteenth birthday. The district attorney's office held that the seriousness of the crime required charging Brandon McInerney as an adult. It is significant that in the discussions surrounding the murder, both adolescents, ages fourteen and fifteen, were transposed into adults because of behavior that children ostensibly don't engage in: hatred culminating in murder in Brandon's case and "cross-dressing" in Latisha's case. In each instance, the behaviors themselves were understood to be evidence that neither child was, in fact, still a child.

In this context I want to return to the press coverage in order to think a bit more about another inversion or erasure that is at the heart of this story. How might race complicate these reports? During the criminal trial, race was deemed to have played no part in the shooting and therefore the narratives emerging from both prosecution and defense were strangely denuded of race, although some of the press coverage did allude to it. Consider this statement from the *Ventura County Star*: "Prosecutors allege it was a hate crime because King wore female clothing

and told classmates he was gay. Authorities allege McInerney held white supremacist views."[9] To follow a statement
about Larry's queerness with a statement about Brandon's
racial hatred creates a strange non sequitur. Despite the
parallel deployment of these signifiers, no part of this article, or any other that the press has written about the case
insofar as I can tell, does the work of connecting these two
facts, or attempts to explain how, precisely, Brandon's racial hatred is inflamed by Larry's queerness. We are left
to infer that the two are related by association or analogy,
that Brandon's white supremacist views would be understood to expand beyond racial hatred to many other kinds
or categories of hatred. Or still more specifically that the
two are related by the transitive property: if the two facts
are understood to be comprehensible in relation to one
another, it is because sexual orientation is understood to
be *like* racial identity in some way, or that they similarly
mark a subject as a target of discrimination and violence.
At issue here are the ways in which asserting sexual identity and racial identity as analogous or transitive is a way
of demonstrating a logical equivalence, leading readers to
conclude that sexual and racial identity are not the same
but are similarly targeted by hatred. The fallacy is that the
logical equivalence forces a false choice, and a binary one,
in identifying the factors that led to the murder. That is,
the assertion appears to be that homophobic violence is
working *like* racial violence, but that comparison requires
racial violence to be invoked in a purely instrumental way,
and then immediately dropped out of the discourse.

One demonstration of this equivalencing comes from
a statement made in one of the pretrial hearings in an-
ticipation of the murder trial itself. As described in the
Star: "A gang expert testified that McInerney was deeply

entrenched in white supremacist ideology, which became the driving force behind the shooting, he said. King was gay and was perceived by McInerney as an enemy of the white race because of his gay lifestyle, according to police Detective Dan Swanson."[10] So: McInerney is charged with a hate crime, and a gang expert testifies that McInerney is part of a white supremacist group. The turn in the above sentence is jarringly strange, where "gay" comes to occupy the place in the sentence where we would expect "not white" to be and where a hatred of gays is *implicitly rendered analogous to* a hatred of nonwhites. But the very strangest thing about this is that *Latisha King was herself biracial and identified as black*, a fact that was rarely mentioned in the press coverage, or in the murder trial. In the representation of this murder in which a white supremacist junior high school student kills a black classmate, race is literally unmentionable and is erased from the story in order to make the narrative about gayness more legible, a legibility that is in turn dependent on the simultaneous analogy with and erasure of trans identity. Race and gender are then bound in a particularly tight paradox, simultaneously offered, on the one hand, as an undifferentiated conglomeration of difference whose relation to each other and to external forces are entirely transitive and, on the other, as a zero-sum game in which the assertion of one threatens to undo the legibility or coherence of the other.

IV. THE BANAL ARTS: ERWIN STRAUS AND THE PHENOMENOLOGY OF WALKING

How might it be possible to see the conditions under which a narrative of homophobic or transphobic violence becomes coherent, at what places it fails to cohere, and what different guises aggression can take in such narratives? I want to suggest that an understanding of bodily movement is paramount to understanding how, in the transphobic logic on display in this trial, gender expression becomes transformed into sexual aggression.

One unlikely ally in this inquiry into social meaning as given through bodily movement is Erwin Straus, a phenomenologist and neurologist who is probably most frequently encountered today in Iris Marion Young's path breaking "Throwing like a Girl." As a work of feminist phenomenology, this essay gets its title and fodder for its trenchant critique of phenomenology's treatment of women and the feminine from Straus's 1952 piece "The Upright Posture," originally published in his volume *Phenomenological Psychology*. I will not take up Young's critique here, not because I don't think it is right or compelling: it is certainly both. What I would like to do instead is to read Straus's essay "The Upright Posture" as offering an exemplary descriptive phenomenology that is particularly useful for describing bodily movement in the performance of gender.

I would to like to consider how phenomenology of this kind, which, following Husserl, we might call a "descriptive and non-idealizing discipline," might help us to apprehend bodies in times, places, and contexts other than Straus's own.[11] That is to say, leaving aside the question of whether Straus's account is sexist—or even tabling the certainty that it is—I want to suggest we might read past that gender bias to ask what tools such a phenomenological method might offer to all sorts of situations, even a situation in which gender is fundamentally at issue.

Straus is worth reconsidering in this case because he gives us perhaps the most thorough phenomenological account we have of the act of walking. Here is how he describes it:

> Human bipedal gait is a rhythmical movement whereby, in a sequence of steps, the whole weight of the body rests for a short time on one leg only. The center of gravity has to be swung forward. . . . Human gait is, in fact, a continually arrested falling. Therefore an unforeseen obstacle or a little unevenness of the ground may precipitate a fall. Human gait is an expansive motion, performed in the expectation that the leg brought forward will ultimately find solid ground. It is motion on credit. Confidence and timidity, elation and depression, and stability and insecurity are all expressed in gait. Bipedal gait is, in fact, a balance alternating from one leg to the other, it permits variations in length, tempo, direction and accent.[12]

The emphasis here is on variation. The movement of walking is generated by a body creating an imbalance in itself that it then corrects over and over again. More crucially still, Straus is naming the wide range of mental and emotional states such variation and repetition can express. But Straus does not begin the essay with walking, just as the human walker does not. "The Upright Posture" begins with a description of a body that is not even able to keep itself upright. "A breakdown of physical well-being is alarming; it turns our attention to functions that, on good days, we take for granted. A healthy person does not ponder about breathing, seeing, walking. Infirmities of breath, sight or gait startle us."[13] He is not trying to describe illness here as much as he is endeavoring to show how illness can disrupt our seamless enmeshment with the world, "a breaking with the typicality of the world," which we will explore in the next chapter. This disruption, he says, causes us to "ponder" what normally we simply, or not so simply, live. On a good day, neither our breath nor our sight nor our gait—and he deliberately lists them in that order—none of those things is present to us; we do not engage them through thinking, and they are not features of our consciousness. That ordering of days in terms of the quality of their embodiment, some good and some bad, is his acknowledgement that infirmity, the "breakdown of physical well-being," as he puts it, is a nearly universal experience. The "we" that he invokes take those functions for granted, but only on good days. What Straus opens with, however, is not a sense of continuity and community with similarly vulnerable bodily others, but rather of strangeness, of being startled, of feeling wary of and put off by that infirmity. Note the equivocation in the referent of that "us," which shifts suddenly. The "us" seemed to be continuous with the "we" who have bodies, but by the second sentence, it is designating a different group. "Among the patients consulting a psychiatrist, there are some who can no longer master the seemingly banal arts of standing and walking."[14]

The "us" who are startled are transported to a scene of patient and psychiatrist, and the assessment of the condition of that patient—who is not paralyzed—aligns the startled "us" with the observing psychiatrist. And it is that observational point of view that characterizes both the doctor and the philosopher in this moment, whose own bodies recede from view as they take up their function as those who attend to other bodies. He continues: "They are not paralyzed, but, under certain conditions, they cannot or feel as if they cannot keep themselves upright."[15] We see here Straus's interest in the psychology of the disorder.

This is confirmed by a difference Straus asserts between not being able to keep oneself upright, and *feeling* that one cannot keep oneself upright. But contrary to the parsing that Straus attempts here, I would insist that a felt sense of incapacity is indistinguishable from incapacity itself. The distinction cannot be a phenomenological one. If I feel that I cannot keep myself upright, as opposed to merely fearing or anticipating that I cannot, then I cannot, in fact, keep myself upright. That distinction—the patient has the capacity to walk but feels he cannot—can be made only from an observational rather than an embodied point of view, since the feeling of the body and its capacity converge in and as the body schema. He goes on to tell us that the significance of the upright posture is psychological and not merely physiological, and describes postural being as the site at which the relation between psychology and physiology can be clearly seen. "Obviously, upright posture is not confined to the technical problems of locomotion. It contains a psychological element. It is pregnant with meaning not exhausted by the physiological tasks of meeting the forces of gravity and maintaining equilibrium."[16] The upright posture is not just about the physical body, but about its interaction with that "psychological element" that renders the posture pregnant with meaning. It is a meaning not exhausted by the physiological tasks of action, and thus not coextensive with the physiology through which it is experienced.

But before the body has even arisen into uprightness, language has already taken up that meaning. "To be upright has two connotations. First to rise, to get up and to stand on one's own feet and second the moral implication, not to stoop to anything, to be honest and just, to be true to friends in danger. To stand by one's convictions and to act accordingly, even at the risk of one's life."[17] For Straus the meanings and indeed the *moral valuations* that we attach to uprightness spread into language. Straus insists on the psychological as an interpenetration of the physiological and the meaningful, and offers that "the term 'upright' in its moral connotation is more than a mere allegory." Here, that "more" is hard to figure unless we understand it to be referring also to something physical, something inescapably joined with the physicality on which the meaning is modeled.[18] And, importantly, it is only once we get to language and have left the realm of strict physiology, or at least augmented it with language, that the stakes are heightened to the level of life itself.

There are, of course, some troubling moments in the description. When he writes, "There is no doubt that the shape and function of the human body are determined in almost every detail by, and for, the upright posture,"[19] it is hard to read his assertion of the seamlessness of the meshing of the form and function of the body, how little daylight there appears to be between "determined by" and "determined for" in that sentence, without hearing Iris Marion Young in our ears. But true to the task of descriptive phenomenology, he is interested less in asking *how did we get this way* and more in asking *what is this way that we are?* In a moment both phenomenological and anti-genealogical, he writes: "This writer's interest is in what man is and not in how he supposedly became what he is."[20]

Straus articulates what he calls a "biologically oriented psychology," which, according to him, demonstrates that our experience of the world is necessarily tied to our physical orientation in space and our comportment as we move through it. We "must not forget that upright posture is an indispensable condition of man's self-preservation.

Upright we are, and we experience ourselves in this specific relation to the world. Men and mice do not have the same environment."[21] The stakes of uprightness are self-preservation, are life itself, as he insists more than once. "Upright we are" posits uprightness as a fundamental to our human-ness. This suggestion that uprightness is not able to be dispensed with exists in rather remarkable tension with his clear articulation of standing, and walking, as achievements, even as biologically improbable ones, in the case of walking. Straus describes that tension this way: "Upright posture characterizes the human species. Nevertheless each individual has to struggle to make it truly his own."[22] If standing and walking are fundamental features of the human animal and also those banal arts that might be failed, then the stakes of this artistry, and the consequences of its failure, could not be any higher.[23]

That specter of failure ensures that an individual's relation to uprightness is necessarily a struggle. "Upright posture keeps us waiting. . . . He has to learn it, to conquer it. The acquisition will pass through several phases which, although not completely separate, are sufficiently distinct. Progress is slow. It takes a number of years. This development will be followed here from the getting up, to standing, and finally to walking."[24] The progress toward the upright posture is species-wide, and it is teleological, inevitably aiming ever upward, at the same time that its species-specific characteristic is a certain amount of effort, of labor. So occupied is Straus with the inescapable significance of *work* in the banal arts of getting up, standing, walking that he muses that the significance of sex for the human species is the fact that it lets us stop resisting gravity and lay our bodies down: "Sex remains a form of lying down," he states categorically, comically.[25]

All this, however, takes as its perspective the man who has gotten up, achieved upright posture, and begun walking. The perspective of a child who has not yet quite done so is a different matter. Straus writes:

> In getting up, man gains his standing in the world. The parents are not the only ones who greet the child's progress with joy. The child enjoys no less the triumph of his achievements. The child certainly does not strive for security. Failure does not discourage him. He enjoys the freedom gained by the upright posture—the freedom to stand on his own feet and the freedom to walk upright. The upright posture, which we learn in and through falling, remains threatened by falls throughout our lives.[26]

The child is untroubled by the prospect of falling. The exuberance of childhood that propels one toward walking, the drive to master it through repeated failures, means that the child must not be deterred by the fear of falling if he is ever to walk. Acquisition of the skill of walking is made possible only in the face of this falling that is not feared, even when it happens, and happens again. As he learns to walk, stumbles, and falls, tries again, falls again, the child must comport himself with an unreasonable and unearned hopefulness about the success of his future efforts. He does so, at least in part, because walking brings the world to him, brings him things in the guise of his bringing himself to them. He does not fear that his reach for mastery will exceed his grasp, even when he should. But the child does experience a fear of and fascination with the objects that walking brings into his path. The man who walks feels confronted by those objects by virtue of his placing himself before them; "he finds himself always 'confronted' with things" in Straus's words.[27] The primary intentionality of our motor orientation toward the world means that we attribute a kind of agency, or a looking back, into the objects we survey.

In his delineation of childhood acquisition of motility Straus articulates a teleology to an ever-straighter uprightness, but the goal is attained only if the walk is of a certain kind, has a certain character. A walk that is not sufficiently "dignified," to use one of his terms, or perhaps one that is not sufficiently upright, sufficiently straight, means that the body is not making good on the species progress toward ever-greater uprightness. The walk and the upright posture are expressive in many ways, and one of those ways, Straus tells us, is sexual. The example that Straus gives describing the sexual expressiveness of the body is worth close attention. We are given a tableau consisting of a man and a woman and a moment of sexual meaning conveyed through the body:

> There is only one vertical but many deviations from it, each one carrying a specific, expressive meaning. The sailor pulls his cap askew, and his girl understands well the cocky expression and his "leanings."[28]

This scene of sexual communication between a man and a woman, a sailor and a girl, hinges around his bodily movement, the sailor pulling his cap askew. Straus will insist that we do not ever have to be *instructed* in how to read such a situation, that "without ever being taught, we understand the rules governing this and other areas of expression. We understand them not conceptually but, it seems, by intuition."[29] Straus offers the example to explain the eloquence of gesture, to show how meaning inheres in the sailor's movements, that his meaning is instantly readable from his posture, that the girl understands both the "expression" of his cap askew, his gesture, and also his "leanings." Bodily materiality is central to the communication of meaning, yet is not in itself sufficient to the meaning aimed at in this example. That is, this aspires to be an explanation of bodily posture, but the expressiveness of the body in this moment is achieved only through the bodily auxiliary of the cap.

Perhaps the most startling thing about this particular example, as we read and understand it today, is that although the sailor's girl may be perfectly clear on the meaning of that cap pulled askew, we as readers may not be. I myself am not clear at all; to my eye that cocked hat is more likely to conjure Tom of Finland than it is to telegraph a heterosexual sailor with his girl or on the make, and the connotative dimension of that word "leanings" does nothing to lean my interpretation toward the latter image rather than the former. The divergence between my reading and Straus's may only demonstrate the danger of understanding the object to be singularly possessing its own meaning, and thus emphasize the necessity of understanding that meaning as always relationally constituted. It shows, too, that the meaning of a gesture might multiply if we understand it in differently gendered or sexualized or racialized contexts. "Thinking about gestures," Juana María Rodríguez writes, "compels us to think about how our racialized, sexualized bodies propel themselves in the world."[30]

V. LOOKING AT AND LOOKING FOR "HOMOSEXUALITY IN AMERICA"

If the tilt of the sailor's cap is a kind of persuasive discourse, then it will succeed in persuading only if the girl knows what it is suggesting. The tilt of the cap will not signify in the same way to every onlooker. Indeed, the girl may be perfectly clear on what the sailor means with the skew of that cap, and she may be perfectly wrong. We might imagine a scene in which the girl misrecognizes the tilt of the cap as her sailor soliciting her, rather than, say, another male sailor, cap also askew, standing right behind her.

With that context in place, we might return to Straus's contention that men and mice do not have the same environment, because their postures are different. They do not inhabit space in the same way; therefore they cannot inhabit the same space. If we could extend this already extended metaphor, or perhaps more properly contract it, might it help us consider what happens when members of the same species have postural variations that make them take up space in fundamentally different ways? If a man and a mouse cannot be said to have the same environment, what about a man and a woman? That last was, of course, Iris Marion Young's challenge to Straus. My query here is similarly oriented but slightly askew: What about a man and a gay man? Or a white not-quite-adult and a mixed-race not-really-boy? Or a boy and a transgirl? What happens when we consider the postulate of a different environment for the differently comported conjugated through queer movement or trans gender? Or to use Straus's own words, how might we think through the notion of "inclination, which just like leaning, means 'bending out' from the austere vertical" in a contemporary context where "inclination" names the direction or course of one's sexual desire?[31] Into what service is a walk or an upright posture pressed when examining the behaviors of those who might also bend in other ways?

As we have seen, the walk is an elaborate and complex expression of embodied life, a rhythmic destabilization and reassertion of the vertical that propels us through the world, toward other people or away from them. But embodied life also offers less elaborated deviations from the vertical, styles of bodily presentation that might function as a signal to others, to bring them into proximity or to keep them at a distance. Let's return to Straus's sailor. Straus explains that the sailor's inclinations are communicated by his cap—that the expression of a gendered style can only be read, and can be universally read, as expressing a sexual advance. His "leaning" does not inhere in the cap itself, but is communicated by how he wears it, the style of its wearing, the angle at which he sets it across his brow. This angle, the physical tilt that indicates an immaterial lean, is understood to be a sign of homosexuality; it is a code evincing a surprising cultural breadth and tenacity, Straus's unfamiliarity with it notwithstanding. The convention—that a cap or a scarf worn precisely askew, cocked or tied on the slant—is apparently longstanding enough in American gay culture to have been referenced in the first mainstream magazine article to document "homosexual life" in 1964, and persistent enough that forty-five years later Larry's teachers could communicate their reading of his sexuality by describing his scarf as "jauntily tied," where once again the angle of the tie is more crucial in determining how the scarf and its wearing are read than any physical attribute of the scarf itself.

Two years before the publication of Straus's "The Upright Posture," *Life* magazine published that essay, "Homosexuality in America." This piece, illustrated with photographs, documents the homosexual underground for the consumption of a heterosexual public assumed to be unaware of such a world. One of the venues described is a bar in the "warehouse district" of San Francisco in 1964. The patrons are leathermen, and the scene is described as conveying a certain amount of menace. One of the most noticeable things about the men described are the caps that they wear. Those caps, or covers, are prominent in the images of the men in the bar, and also figure in magazine's descriptions of their masculinity. The leathermen in the unnamed bar are described this way: "The effort of these homosexuals to appear manly is obsessive—in the rakish angle of the caps, in the thumbs boldly hooked in belts."[32] As described, the accessorizing marks and enhances a certain kind of masculinity, but also detracts from it in implying that excessive attention to dress and presentation necessarily slants that presentation toward the feminine. An over-concern with physical appearance, it is implied, queers even the most hyperbolically masculine gender, turns the unselfawareness that is the hallmark of masculinity into preening or dandyishness.

Each aspect of this dressing and accessorizing is freighted with meaning, in ways that are not always entirely apparent to a casual observer, even as it is implied that the language of gesture that governs the donning of those accessories is universal. An angle is always "rakish," or in Latisha's case, "jaunty," rather than crooked or sloppy. Thumbs are hooked in belts "boldly," though it is unclear what exactly it is that is bold about the gesture of a thumb crooked around a belt loop. These leathermen are portrayed as having an obsessive relation to their own manliness, but the article also introduces us to homosexuals who do not, who are described as "swishy" and "effeminate." These two groups of homosexuals are differentiated in terms of gender, the obsessively manly leathermen versus the effeminate softness of the boys in Chelsea and the Village, the opposed textures of California SM culture (leather) and Chelsea boys (fluffy). While some of the photographic illustrations purport to show the shadowy world of homosexuals that the world of heterosexuals could not possibly fathom, other photographs portray homosexuals as they move through the straight world, and are encountered by heterosexuals. Indeed, the crux of the article is about those encounters between the heterosexual and homosexual worlds, where the index of the visibility homosexual world is a measure of its visibility to straights, and its increasing visibility is seen as fundamentally *about* heterosexuality, an aggressive movement out toward it.

The article also offers two photographs depicting the world of more effeminate gays. The first shows the torso of mannequin displayed in a storefront window. He is dressed in a jacket and a long plaid scarf, one arm is crossed protectively over his midsection, and the other arm reaches up across the chest, one finger of the masculine hand resting on the collarbone in a delicately feminine pose. On his head is an outrageously oversized hat. The caption reads: "The window of this New York Greenwich village store which caters to homosexuals is filled with the colorful, offbeat attention-calling clothes that the 'gay' world likes."[33] The store window solicits our attention, and it does so, by implication, in the same way that homosexuals solicit our attention, with color, exaggeration, outrageousness. As in the description of Latisha King's feminine attire, so here the agency is given to the clothing itself; it is the clothing itself that procures the attention that the homosexual is understood to crave.

This characterization of homosexuals as craving and demanding attention is another remarkably persistent stereotype, and it played a central role in the trial. One of Latisha's teachers, Anne Sinclair, gave testimony about the ways in which she understood Latisha to have been engaging in "negative attention seeking." She explained that this seeking of attention was something that could be felt the moment Latisha entered a room. Merely the entrance itself, in Sinclair's view, was a demand for attention, because of the way in which Latisha entered that room. And since the attention she received in school was almost invariably negative attention, Latisha was necessarily demanding bad attention. That demand for attention was described as bodily but non-verbal. She "announces" through her manner of entering a room and her style of dress, both of which are described by Defense Attorney Robyn Bramson as "flamboyant," a word Bramson offers to the teacher, who affirms it in a string of assent. "Flamboyant," here and elsewhere, functions as a cipher for "homosexual" when the latter cannot be uttered.

BRAMSON: And you've described him as dramatic?
SINCLAIR: Yes.
BRAMSON: Coming into a room?
SINCLAIR: Yes.
BRAMSON: Announcing his presence?
SINCLAIR: Yes.
BRAMSON: And that he became a bit more flamboyant as well?
SINCLAIR: Yes.
BRAMSON: Would that be a good word?
SINCLAIR: Yes.
BRAMSON: In his style of dress?
SINCLAIR: Yes. [34]

Latisha, by all accounts, was a large presence. She knew how to enter a room. She liked to be noticed. She knew how to work it. If we read this form of embodied movement as a demand, the question then becomes: What is this a demand for? And what is being extracted from whom? Sinclair understands it to be a demand that others give Latisha negative attention; Latisha is demanding an unhappy engagement with the other. In this view, if others then react with unhappiness, negativity, or aggression, they are only acceding to what Latisha herself has demanded.

BRAMSON: Why you would say that he engaged in negative attention-seeking behavior?

SINCLAIR: Well, I was going to say I was always aware when he came into the classroom. I mean, it's not like—if I wasn't looking at the door, I mean, I would know that he had entered the room. I mean, some kids can quietly come into the room, and other kids kind of bring more attention to themselves when they come into the room.

BRAMSON: And you felt that Larry brought more attention to himself?

SINCLAIR: Right.[35]

What was occluded in this exchange between the defense attorney and the teacher was the teacher's own look, her own desire to look. We can read a hint of it in that breaking off, her saying "I mean, it's not like—" and not finishing the sentence. What follows is her contention that she was not looking at the door when Latisha came in. The words that are swallowed prior to that demurral cannot be read, as we are left with only the negative imprint of the thing about to be conjured ("it's not like") followed by the impossibility of its formulation. It's not like she was looking at the door before Latisha came in. *It's not like she wanted to look.* Latisha made her do it.

With this we see another troubling consequence of understanding the performance of non-normative gender as a demand for attention, but also some of the dangers of reading the performance of gender as a demonstration of agency. If it is Latisha's own demand that draws Sinclair's looks toward the door, then Latisha's demand provides cover for Sinclair's own desire to look and to see. Sinclair is not responsible for acknowledging or attending to her own desire. The attribution of "negative attention seeking" to Latisha means that the scene is a story of Latisha's agency, rather than a story of Sinclair's own desire to look, which is both satisfied and occluded by her turn toward Latisha.

The *Life* magazine piece also tells a story, or several, about the complex circuits of desire and disgust, recognition and retraction, that are at play when straight people look at queer people. One of the photographs shows two couples passing each other as they walk through what looks to be Washington Square Park. The first couple appears to be two young men, and the camera captures them from the back in the left of the frame as they walk away from us. Walking toward them and toward the viewer is a second couple, a middle-aged woman and a balding man. The first couple is looking straight ahead. The second couple is looking at the first, the man with a hard, sizing-up stare, and the woman with a not-quite-legible gaze. There is a shadow between her brows, and a hint of flare and raise in her nostrils. Her look may be unkind; it may be curious. It may be compassionate, it may be fearful. The most readable aspect of her embodiment is not her face but her hands. One white-gloved hand clutches her pocketbook and the other clutches her husband, curling around his elbow. His hands are unreadable, pushed into the pockets of his pants, but his face is anything but inscrutable. His brow is furrowed, his eyes are narrowed, his stare is hard, and his tongue is pushed into his lower lip. It is a look of judgment, of disapproval, of contempt.

The photograph's caption reads: "Two fluffy-sweatered young men stroll in New York City, ignoring the stare of a 'straight' couple. Flagrant homosexuals are unabashed by reactions of shock, perplexity, disgust."[36] The caption indicates that the photograph captures homosexuals' desire and their flagrancy, even as the only physical evidence of desire captured by the photograph is the desire of the straight couple to look at the gay one. The young men are looking ahead, not returning the openly hostile stare that is directed at them. They walk through the park, side by side but not touching. Their sweaters are soft, as are the stances; the young man closest to the center of the frame is slightly contrapposto, caught mid-stride in the play of balance that is human bipedal gait. Each has his arms closed protectively around his own torso, contained, containing. They are not soliciting attention in their comportment; their bodies evidencing rather the opposite, a kind of proprioceptive retraction. Nor their gazes: straight ahead, slightly down, non-challenging. Yet is the homosexual couple who are characterized as seeking attention, soliciting stares, flagrantly and brazenly courting the attention of the straight couple in a characterization that can free the slack-jawed onlookers from having to face their own desire to look. With the insistence that homosexuals are "unabashed" by the "shock, perplexity, disgust" of the onlooker, the chief complaint against these homosexuals is advanced: not that they are violating norms of gender or sexual behavior, but that they are doing so without a sufficient sense of shame, a charge whose workings in this case I have explored elsewhere.[37]

VI. THE TURN

The period of time between classes allotted to the students to walk from one classroom to another is called the "passing period." The day before the shooting, there was an incident during the passing period that was, according to Dr. Hoagland, the defense psychologist, "the trigger incident" in the case. Brandon recounted that he was walking along the hallway with his friend Keith L. and saw Latisha approaching, walking down the hallway. Brandon then bent the arc of his path wide, veering away from Latisha. In Brandon's telling, he was trying to steer clear of Latisha. Dr. Hoagland said: "He was not wanting any trouble. He tried to avoid him. They passed each other and then the defendant turned around and looked at him and the victim said something." The victim said something but no one was certain what it was. Brandon did not hear the words. His friend Keith did not hear the words. Brandon heard only the word at the end: "baby." After the shooting, he said that Latisha might have said: "What's up, baby?" Or that she might have said: "What's wrong, baby?" Brandon was not sure. He could not remember exactly what was said. This incident was, according to the defense, the defining moment in the case. Latisha called Brandon "baby," and according to Brandon, this was disgusting, the worst thing anyone had ever said to him. "I have never been disrespected like that," he said.

Dr. Hoagland is asked why such a seemingly innocuous comment would be reacted to in such a violent manner: "Was it the comment, what was it about this incident that upset Brandon?" Dr. Hoagland responds: "There are multiple things. One was that this boy who was dressing as a woman and secondarily who was gay that was coming up and saying these kinds of provocative things to him in front of many other people. I think Brandon said that was the straw that popped the balloon." Which was indeed how Brandon described his feelings after the incident, "the final straw that popped the balloon," mixing the metaphor in order that he not be the camel with a broken back, but rather the balloon popping, a noise that several of the children thought they heard that morning in the classroom, and only realized, once they smelled gunpowder and saw Brandon standing over Latisha body aiming to fire a second shot into her head, that it was not a balloon at all.

Brandon agreed with Dr. Hoagland's assessment that it was Latisha's gender transgression, rather than her sexual orientation, that provoked him toward violence. The gender transgression was primary, and Latisha's sexual orientation was only "secondary." "I knew he was gay," Brandon said "but he took it to a whole other level. What the hell, high heels and makeup and hairdo? It was surprising and disgusting." Brandon, in fact, was quite precise in articulating that his hatred of Latisha stemmed from the fact that she was violating gender roles. When Prosecutor Fox asked the psychologist, "Did you talk to him about why he found it so disgusting?" Hoagland responded: "Yes. He said that it was such a disruption of what was expected from a male that simply seeing that was upsetting and disturbing."

The events of the "trigger incident," however, deserve a second look. Brandon and Latisha pass each other in the hall, apparently without incident. No words are exchanged, nothing is reported. After they have passed one another, Brandon reports that he turns to look at Latisha. Brandon turns to look. He does not say why. We do not know what motivated that look. It was not words between them. It was not physical contact. It was not, so far as anyone can tell, anything that Latisha did. For some reason after they have walked past one another, Brandon turns around to look at Latisha. And what he reports about that moment is that Latisha is looking at him. Latisha's look is one that Brandon would not have perceived had he not turned around and looked himself, so it is only his own act of turning and looking that allows Latisha's look to emerge, and offers him as receptive to Latisha's look. The "triggering incident" begins with some desire of Brandon's, a desire that oriented his body back and behind, as he turned himself toward Latisha. He is hailed in the moment after he has turned to look, with an unheard utterance and the word "baby." If we are to understand the disgust, the revulsion, the blinding rage that Brandon reports feeling at this moment, we must realize that it is not just a reaction to Latisha's half-heard utterance, but also a reaction to Brandon's own turn, his own solicitation of that utterance with his body and his look.

o o o

During the murder trial, the court is half-full of people: the lawyers, the jury, the gallery, the accused—all eyes to the judge. The entrance is in the back of the courtroom. As I am sitting in the gallery and listening to the proceedings, transcribing the testimony into my laptop as quickly as I am able, I hear the squeak of the hinge of the double door behind me open as someone enters the courtroom.

And Brandon turns around. I keep listening, it keeps squeaking, he keeps turning. When court is in session and that door opens with a squeak, and a bailiff or a witness or a family member enters the courtroom, Brandon turns around in his chair. Every time. He swivels his head around with his face to the gallery to see who has entered, then quickly turns back around to face front. It is as if the sound and the feeling of someone coming in and standing behind him is unbearable. That feeling of being the object of someone's gaze, a someone whom he cannot see, shifts him and turns him around in his chair. When he turns around to face the door, he rearranges his body with the turn, insuring that he is not in the same position relative to whoever is entering the room that Latisha was when Brandon shot her: seated, blind from behind, her back and the back of her head offering themselves as one target.

2

MOVEMENT

There is a story that came out around, I don't know, eight years ago. Of a young man who lived in Maine and he walked down the street of his small town where he had lived his entire life. And he walks with what we would call a swish, a kind of, his hips move back and forth in a feminine way. And as he grew older that swish, that walk, became more pronounced, and it was more dramatically feminine. He started to be harassed by the boys in the town, and soon two or three boys stopped his walk and they fought with him and they ended up throwing him over a bridge and they killed him. So then we have to ask: why would someone be killed for the way they walk? Why would that walk be so upsetting to those other boys that they would feel that they must negate this person, they must expunge the trace of this person. They must stop that walk no matter what. They must eradicate the possibility of that person ever walking again. It seems to me that we are talking about an extremely deep panic or fear or anxiety that pertains to gender norms. . . . Someone says: you must comply with the norm of masculinity otherwise you will die. Or I kill you now because you do not comply.
—Judith Butler, *Judith Butler: Philosophical Encounters of the Third Kind* (2006)

The spirit of the world is ourselves, as soon as we know how to move and look.
—Merleau-Ponty, "Indirect Language and the Voices of Silence"

I. BREAKING THE TYPICALITY OF THE WORLD

A shock is something that happens that causes us to shift our interpretation and understanding of an event in our world. Such an event seems actually to change the nature of the world around us, breaking our modes of understanding, our habits of seeing, our ways of hearing. Fred Moten describes the ways in which a shock, a break, is an alteration of representation itself, a disturbance that reconfigures the visual and aural registers. His book *In the Break* describes how shocks and breaks shape and break and shape meaning, how collusion and disarticulation between sound and image break and fracture in the face of racist violence. Moten recalls the example of a child whose death represents just such a break, the representation of whose death offers the "the shock of the shock" in Moten's words.[1] This is another black child, also accused of being precocious. Of wanting to be the center of attention. Of bringing trouble on himself. He was accused of going too far. Moten's invocation is of Emmett Till, who was alleged to have whistled at a white woman and uttered the phrase "Bye, baby" as he was leaving a store, an offence for which he was lynched.[2] Till's death and its aftermath enacted a fracture between sound and image. We can see a similar fracture in the King case. One can think of the spectacle that was made of Latisha's embodiment in the school, the ways in which the visual aspect of Latisha's embodiment blotted out the aural one. Latisha's name was almost never uttered, not at the school, not during the trial. The privileging of the visual over the auditory rendered the nearly constant stream of slurs, of hostile commentary, of "fag," of denigration directed at Latisha by the other students inaudible. It was not part of the official story, did not register as significant. The consequence of this privileging meant that unlike all of the visual provocation that was ostensibly so central to the case—the ways in which Latisha's dress, hair, and mannerisms, whether recalled or imagined, were described in such minute detail—the words constituting the "trigger incident" also did not land in the register, either of the trial or of collective memory. It was a single word—"baby"—with other words proximate to it, which was considered to be the provocation. The other words surrounding that one word refused to contribute any sense to the sentence, acting as blank containment rather than offering meaning. In the end, the words themselves vanished, as we saw in the last chapter.

We can also turn to phenomenology for an articulation of shock and the ways in which it breaks the representational frame. One definition is Alfred Schütz's, who describes shock as "a radical modification in the tension of our consciousness."[3] In his monograph on Schütz, Maurice Natanson describes a shock as "the condition which occasions a shift from one finite province [of meaning] to another."[4] This feeling of a jarring and unexpected shift, of a bump on the road that throws us, that veers us from our path, is the beginning of the constitution and reconstitution of meaning. That shift is also a way of describing what phenomenology is. Richard Zaner describes phenomenology in just this way, also borrowing from Schütz to characterize it: when going along with our daily lives something will happen, a small mundane something that will "shock you into an awareness of what you had been taking for granted all along."[5] It is shock that makes us assess the situation before us, makes us begin thinking where previously we had merely been moving along, motoring forward, inattentively. We suddenly are thrown by the shock into thought and thus are tasked with rethinking. The shock initiates the re-arrival of the self to consciousness. Shock condemns the self to reflection on its circumstances and world, a reflection that can be described as either the method or practice of phenomenology.

What we often feel as we shift from one interpretation of an event to another is a vertiginous unsettling. It is the feeling of having our habitual and familiar experience of the world suddenly snapped. This is how many of the teachers at E. O. Green Junior High School describe their experiences with Latisha. In her appearance, her mannerisms, her comportment, she was a radical affront to their assessment of how a boy should look and behave, and also of what constituted a girl. The sound of her walk occasioned a break in the familiar everydayness of the school, even as it became familiar enough to identify her through sound alone. Larry was not a typical boy, and Latisha was not a typical girl; her failure to conform to the expected norms and rules of gendered behavior had an ambiguous and pervasive effect within the school. Her walk, in particular, was a break with, and in, typicality itself. To those who saw Latisha as a willful agent and her gender as an expression of that will, she refused to adopt the mantle of typicality. Those who understand gender norms to be something other than the chosen or refused attributes of a willing subject might phrase it otherwise, saying that Latisha did not embody "boyhood" in a way that they thought a boy ought to, yet they could not quite conceive of her embodiment as a girlhood. It was illegible as such to those around her. When dealing with Latisha, her teachers seem to have experienced this breaking with typical behavior as a breaking of the typicality of the world itself.

II. THE SIMPLE CLICK OF HER HEEL
ON THE GROUND

In his essay "Indirect Language and the Voices of Silence," Maurice Merleau-Ponty describes the ways in which perception is always a stylization of what is perceived. Perception opens the object up to us, often through a flicker of an image, a single sound, or a gesture. Merleau-Ponty is talking about painting in this essay, but gives several examples of perceptions opening up the perceived object in which that disclosure happens in the auditory rather than the visual realm. In explaining how perception opens something up for us, in an instant, he writes this: "A woman passing by is not first and foremost a corporeal contour for me, a colored mannequin, or a spectacle; she is 'an individual, sentimental, sexual expression.' She is a certain manner of being flesh which is given entirely in her walk or even in *the simple click of her heel on the ground*, just as the tension of the bow is present in each fiber of wood—a most remarkable variant of the norm of walking, looking, touching, and speaking that I possess in my self-awareness because I am a body."[6] This is the body in its sexual being, this woman passing by, apprehended as such by Merleau-Ponty's "I" who is also a body. She is not, he says, apprehended visually. She not a spectacle, not a mannequin. The visual fact of her materiality does not express her being. We might hear an echoed refutation of Descartes here and his skeptical distrust of both the body and the senses: How do we know who or what is under those hats and cloaks we see walking about in the street? Could be heads of pumpkin or glass, could be automatons. Nonsense, says Merleau-Ponty. The walk is disclosive of being itself. It is not that I see the woman walking, catch a glimpse of her, and then know some aspect of her. I know her entire being, which is "given entirely in her walk or even the simple click of her heel on the ground." It is a grasping of the other that is instantaneous and total, in which the visual register is incidental. It is the sound itself, the sound of her walking, through which her being is entirely given.

And what, precisely, *is* that sound? It might be characterized first and foremost by its precision. It is the sound of gender *as* precision. Merleau-Ponty uses the word *choc*, which has been translated variously as "click"[7] and "shock": "the simple shock of her heel on the ground."[8] Both click and shock invoke a resonating, a reverberation, a way in which a singular moment—the noise of a heel striking the ground—becomes what it is through a repetition, gaining its meaning as one footfall follows another follows another, thus transforming a single noise into the rhythmic pattern of motion given through sound. That one singular sound also echoes, as well as non-singularly repeating, gathering evocation and meaning and significance in its wake. "Indirect Language and the Voices of Silence" is an essay about painting and also about language, in which Merleau-Ponty makes the case that painting can be approached, interpreted, understood, and analyzed like a language.[9] The voices of painting, he says, are the voices of silence.[10] It is at the same time an essay about gesture; gesture is the key to every articulation of meaning that the essay wants to describe.

We will return to the question of gesture and silence and turn to those moments in the trial when the former comes to fill in the latter, becoming a way to convey what is otherwise unspeakable. But we might first consider: What is the nature of gesture? Is there some element that unifies gesture across the visual, auditory, and discursive realms? How does a gesture coalesce into a habit? Or become articulated as a style?

III. THE SHOCK OF GENDER

Brandon was seventeen in the summer of 2011, when the murder trial began. The trial offered many descriptions of the actions of Brandon McInerney before the morning of February 13. But it was equally invested, perhaps more so, in describing the actions of Latisha King. The proceedings were *ab initio* as much about establishing what kind of person Latisha King was as they were concerned with what kind of person Brandon McInerney was. And in this, it was a trial with a fundamental stake and interest in reading, decoding, parsing, and enacting the gestures of the human body.

Indeed, most of the contestation in the murder trial orbited around bodily gestures: how to read them, how to determine what they express, how to interpret what they mean. In this chapter, I examine how Latisha's gestures were interpreted and will read several moments when gender fractured into separate auditory and visual registers, each with different modes of action and effects. This fracture happened in the school, as Latisha walked down the hallway, and it also happened in the courtroom, as the defense attorneys made their arguments. In the former, gender became an attribute of sound, as the testimony of many teachers made clear in their extreme reaction to the sound of that walk. In the latter, the meaning-making functions of the auditory register were supplemented and eventually replaced by the visual register as the attorneys attempted to portray Latisha's gender and sexuality through gesture. Argumentation in a courtroom is necessarily an auditory affair, made through testimony, offered through examination and cross-examination, through the workings of spoken language. What I will explore here are the moments in which, during this trial, the defense attorneys made their arguments through gesture. That is: at moments in the trial when language failed, when the discourse circled around some formation of gender or sexuality that was unspeakable, that words failed to capture, the wordless language of bodily gesture took over, and meaning was made and transmitted through gesture.

Neither side disputed that Brandon fatally shot Latisha from a distance of about thirty inches away, as she was seated in front of her computer screen, typing her name at the top of the essay she was composing. "Ladies and gentlemen," said District Attorney Maeve Fox in her opening statement, "the evidence will show that this was an execution." She described Brandon's actions before and during the shooting—the quietness with which he rose from his chair in order that Latisha not turn around and see him, how closely Brandon positioned his body to Latisha's, the calm steady way he moved as his arms rose and he pointed the gun at the back of Latisha's head, and his expressionless gaze after he fired two shots. These were the gestures that constituted evidence of Brandon's cold-bloodedness, the "malice aforethought" required for a finding of murder. The defense read those same gestures and concluded that the killing was not murder but manslaughter, that the accused was acting out of panic and that the paradoxically calm and expressionless nature of his gestures were evidence of bodily dissociation and thus emotional distress.

Was it panic or was it an execution? The answer depends on how Brandon's gestures are interpreted. But the gestures that were subject to the greatest scrutiny were not Brandon's, but Latisha's. It was Latisha's walk in particular around which entire days of testimony were organized. One teacher at the school who testified about Latisha's walk, Jill Eckman, said that she was never able to see what Latisha was wearing on her feet, or that she did not remember seeing what she wore. What she did remember was the sound that her boots made when walking down the hallway at school:

> FOX: Outside of the makeup did you notice any other changes in his attire?
> JILL ECKMAN: He started wearing high-heeled boots.
> FOX: Do you remember what they looked like?
> ECKMAN: Not really. I just know they were heels and clicked when he walked down the hall.

Eckman disapproved of his boots, of the sound they made. Other adults were also dismayed by his boots, or angered, or, in the words of other teachers, "shocked," "appalled," and "horrified." In that instance, the sound of the heel striking the ground was shocking because that click, so instantly and recognizably feminine, came from the movement of a body that was not a woman's body. That is, the movement of this body was recognizably feminine although its sex may not have been. And the shock of that discrepancy led to corporeal policing on the part of Latisha's peers, Latisha's teachers, and, especially, Brandon McInerney.

There was something that was readable and legible about Latisha's walk, something that was read as announcing her sexuality through announcing her wayward relation to gender, and that something was conveyed through sound. A walk can convey any number of forms of iconic masculinity; the assertive masculinity of the walk of a soldier, or a cowboy, or a construction worker, is partially expressed in each case through a masculine style of walk that is accompanied by sound, or rather sound is part of what makes the style masculine. The masculinity of each figure is described by movement, and by the sound of movement; one can imagine the sound of soldiers marching in formation, scores of footfalls landing heavily as one, or the jangle of a cowboy's spurs as they strike the planking of a floor.

A walk can also convey femininity through sound. The sound of Latisha's footsteps is recounted throughout the testimony: one teacher described it as a clip-clop, recalling the sound of horses' hooves or of a little girl playing dress-up in shoes too big. But more frequently it is described as a clicking. As we have seen, Merleau-Ponty suggests that the clicking sound that high-heeled shoes make on a hard-surfaced floor is an aural sign of an accomplished femininity. It means the body has trained itself into those shoes, the precision and crispness of the sound speaking to the skill that the wearer has in the wearing, their function as a bodily extension. That extension is not just the physical elongation of the leg accomplished by the height of the heel, but an extension that travels past the visual and into the auditory realm. The click of the heel extends the umbra of femininity out past the body itself, out of reach but within earshot. You could hear him coming, said another teacher, referring to the sound of Latisha's boots.

A few of the teachers at E.O. Green implied that she had no skill in the boots. One opined that she was likely to twist her ankle or break her neck in them. This fantasized ankle-twisting and neck-breaking were offered as a reason to get Latisha to stop wearing the boots; several of the teachers got together and pondered changing the dress code, wondering if they might amend it to prohibit "unsafe" clothing. In insisting that the boots were "a safety issue," the teachers implied a desire to protect Latisha from physical injury resulting from what they understood to be her own ill-chosen game of dress-up carried too far. These teachers, however, were in the minority in their characterization of Latisha's walk in her boots. More of the teachers, and all of the students, described Latisha as being quite skilled in her boots, of walking without wobbling or falling down, of being able to run quickly over bumpy terrain in them, even chasing boys across the playground in them. It is of course possible that both are true—that Latisha began by clip-clopping in those boots, and ended flying across the playground blacktop, that her gendered walk started as ungainly and ended as accomplished, in a fairly brief timespan.

Shirley Brown, a teacher who was "appalled" by Latisha's shoes, was asked why she was appalled. She replied:

BROWN: Well because. Most women have to adjust to the three- or four-inch heel, and here is this child running in them through the grass, potholes and all of that, and it's like what the heck are you doing? And it was like that. Because it's always safety first.

Q: And why did you comment?

BROWN: I always comment to a kid who is sticking himself out in any way, making themselves a target.

Q: Was he sticking out?

BROWN: How could he not?

Brown takes umbrage at the shoes because of how Latisha wears them, "running in them" through all manner of terrain. Her outrage is grounded in the fact that "most women have to adjust to the three- or four-inch heel," and here is this "child" who has apparently adjusted well enough to run through "the grass, potholes, all of that." Latisha, whom she characterizes as a child, is apparently at ease enough in the shoes to wear them confidently, whereas a full grown woman would have had to "adjust" to them. Indeed, her assertion that her concern was "safety first" is belied by her account of how Latisha wore the boots, not just clipping along in them timidly, but running. That question—*what the heck are you doing?*—seems then to address Latisha's gender violation rather than any breach of safety, since the literal answer to the outraged question would be: *I am running quickly across the playground in heels without stumbling or falling down.* One might even read a certain measure of gender envy in Brown's response—an affective cloud around the fact that Latisha's motility in the boots seemed to evince more ease and comfort than most grown women would be able to manage, by her own report. It may or may not be relevant to observe that Shirley Brown delivered this testimony as she sat in the witness box wearing a pair of shoes that had at most perhaps an inch of lift.

Another sensible-shoe wearing teacher, Anne Sinclair, also remarked on those boots, though her recollection of how Latisha wore them was quite different. Sinclair understood Latisha to have been making noise in her boots on purpose, in order to draw attention to herself. This was significant for the defense's attempts throughout the trial to document what they called Latisha's "negative attention-seeking" behaviors. In response to a defense attorney's question as to whether she witnessed Latisha engaged in "negative attention seeking behavior," Sinclair described Latisha in her boots: a spectacle that was auditory rather than visual.

SINCLAIR: Um, he started—well, he started wearing
   boots, high-heeled boots. Very first time I saw the

boots, though, that I remember I believe it was after winter break, we came back to school. I was going across the quad. It was before school started, and I could hear this *click click click click click click click* of heels, and he started yelling, "Mrs. Sinclair, Mrs. Sinclair," and I turned around and he said, "Look at my boots." And he had on knee-high brown suede boots.[11]

Mrs. Sinclair hears her before she sees her. Indeed, to her the sound of the boots signifies an escalation in Latisha's self-presentation, a gestural style of comportment that demands attention in a way that her other, merely visual modes of self-presentation—her nail polish and her hair gel—do not.

DEFENSE ATTORNEY BRAMSON: The manner in which he was dressing and his appearance, did that continue?

ANNE SINCLAIR: Yes.

Q: Did it escalate in any way, or did it stay about the same?

A: I—I—it—he seemed—he seemed bolder about it.

Q: What do you mean?

A: I—when he first started wearing nail polish, he actually kind of covered it up. He pulled his sleeves down of his sweatshirt, and after a while he was just, um, drawing attention, but with the heels you could hear the heels—I mean, you can hear four-inch heels when they're clicking, and he would make sure that they would—that you could hear them clicking as he was walking.

Q: Is there something that you noticed specifically about the way he walked in the heels that led you to believe that he was trying to make the sound of the clicking?

A: Um, well, I believe you can either make noise when you're walking with your shoes or you cannot make noise when you're walking with your shoes, and you could definitely hear the shoes.[12]

The fact that the shoes are audible becomes the fact of Latisha's *intention* to make that noise, to disturb the teachers and the other students. Sinclair's attribution of intention to Latisha was challenged by the district attorney in her cross examination:

ON CROSS, MS. FOX: Now, I was a little confused. On direct exam, you made a couple of statements. One statement was that you believed that Larry had trouble walking in those boots based on your observations, correct?

A: Yes, uh-huh.

Q: But then a minute or two before that you said that it was your opinion that he was walking in a way to make the—the shoes sound loud on purpose?

A: Well—

Q: I don't understand how those two things can co-exist. Can you explain that?

A: Well, I think if you have four-inch heels on and even if you're having trouble walking in them you can still make a lot of noise with them on concrete which is—

Q: That's my point. If you're having trouble walking in them, isn't that inconsistent with purposefully trying to make noise in them? You see what I mean?

A: I think he could have not been as loud as he was, no.

Q: Well, I guess I'm going to ask you to choose then which it is.

A: Okay. Which do I think it is? I do not think he was walking in them like someone who had been walking in them for several—who had practiced a long time. I think they were new to him.

Q: Difficult, correct?

A: Yes. But I also think that you can walk in an exaggerated way which might have also made it difficult for him to be walking without them bothering him, and you can make noise with—you know, certain shoes make more noise than others. I could certainly hear him coming up—I heard him before I saw him. I heard the boots before I saw them.[13]

Fox then switched gears, making a bid for a moment of feminine identification that was surely enhanced by the five-inch heels on her own feet, though they made no sound as she walked back and forth in front of the witness stand in the carpeted cloister of the courtroom.

FOX: Do you have shoes that when you walk they make a lot of noise?

SINCLAIR: Well, I don't wear heels.

Q: That was my very next question.

A: But I have worn heels. At this point in my life, I do—I take comfort over style, okay.

Q: And is it not true, based on your experience back in the day, that when you wear heels, sometimes they are loud regardless of what you do?

A: They can be loud, yes.

Q: It depends on how they fit, correct?

A: Yes.

Q: And you don't know how those shoes fit him, do you?

A: No.

Q: So the opinion that you gave that you think he was purposefully trying to make the shoes sound louder, is that based on anything other than what you have already told us?

A: It's an opinion.

Q: Exactly. And we're here—

A: Okay.

Q: And an opinion is only as good as the information on which it is based. And that is what I'm trying to get at is, do you have any other information than what you have given us that supports that opinion?

A: Okay. They were boots. They weren't strappy little shoes that tend to make more noise. He was wearing boots that were—seemed to fit him or at least being adhering to his—you know, he wasn't sliding around in them. He was wearing boots. They were making noise.

Q: If they fit him and he wasn't sliding around in them, then why did you perceive that they were a safety issue?

A: Well, for one thing, the concrete around our school has really wide cracks, and if you wear those kind of shoes, you can catch your heel in them and you could trip.[14]

When the defense attorneys raise this question of safety, the nature of the danger that Latisha's boots pose is characterized quite differently. Given Sinclair's statement that the boots are dangerous because of the cracks in the concrete around the school, one might wonder why the dress code, and not the cracked concrete, becomes the focus of the anxious huddle of teachers, hand-wringing about "safety." Yet in her answer to Defense Attorney Bramson, Sinclair opines that the boots are dangerous because of the particular kinds of boys around the school—a claim that the defense attorney shuts down as soon as it is uttered, as quickly as she can.

> Q. BY MS. BRAMSON: Do you feel that the way Larry was dressing and behaving was a safety issue?
>
> SINCLAIR: Yes.
>
> Q. BY MS. BRAMSON: Okay. Could you explain that, please?
>
> A: I thought it was a safety issue because I—I felt the boots were unsafe for him any—regardless of whether they were going to allow them or not, that it wasn't safe to be walking around in spike heels at our school. That there's a safety issue there. I also thought it was a safety issue because I—it opens him up to ridicule from other students and that he could get hurt.
>
> Q: By hurt you—
>
> A: Beat up. I assumed he would be beaten up.
>
> MS. BRAMSON: Are we going to break?
>
> THE COURT: How much longer are you going to go?
>
> MS. BRAMSON: I have several minutes. I need to re-group. My back is killing me. I'm asking to break for lunch.
>
> THE COURT: You can sit down and ask questions, but we'll take a break until 1:30.[15]

One of the women who staffed the front office at E. O. Green offers a moment of origin for the boots, relating a story about Latisha first bringing the boots to school. Latisha announced rather proudly that she bought them with her own money, along with two other pairs of shoes. The staffer chastised Latisha for this fact, not on the grounds of gender impropriety, but on the grounds of practicality. It is wasteful, she said, to buy too many shoes at one time. Because who needs that many shoes? And impractical, she said, because children's feet grow quickly. She said, "You won't be able to wear them for very long," which was true, but not because Latisha's feet would ever grow any larger.

IV. GESTURE AND MEANING

In her book *Refiguring the Ordinary*, Gail Weiss uses phenomenology to examine our social interactions with difference and our embodied relations with otherness, and reminds us that perspectives and perceptions are necessarily social phenomena. Weiss emphasizes the importance of gesture to communication and meaning, constructed in what George Herbert Mead calls a "conversation of gestures." She writes:

> By following his argument that perspectives are socially constituted, one can in turn see how the social constitution of perspective depends upon shared horizons and shared social contexts. For Mead, it is in and through everyday participation with others in what he calls a "conversation of gestures" that perspectives as well as selves are constructed. These conversations allow for a variety of meanings to emerge precisely because of the differences in gesture, horizons, context, and perspective that the various interlocutors contribute to the conversation, thereby revealing multiple sources for the ambiguity that both Merleau-Ponty and Beauvoir identify as an essential feature of human experience.[16]

A "conversation of gestures" describes a bodily means of communication that is not fundamentally material, though it engages the materiality of the body and is animated through it. As we saw in chapter 1, in the case of the sailor, his girl, and his ambiguously tilted cap, the conversation can happen face to face. But it need not always.

To understand language, Merleau-Ponty says, we must engage ourselves with its gestures. It is not a matter of moving language aside to tend to the purity of the thoughts there, as if language were a neutral vehicle of meaning. Meaning and its expression are indivisible. As he writes in *The Visible and the Invisible*, "the meaning is not on the phrase like the butter on the bread."[17] It is, rather, a matter of our submitting ourselves to language. "We have only to lend ourselves to its life," he writes, "or its movement, or differentiation and articulation, and to its eloquent gestures."[18] We lend ourselves to the life of language in order to understand it; we give ourselves over to its movement, which is the location of its meaning. Its meaning is not propositional but gestural, expressed in "eloquent gestures." Language "does not stop"; it cannot be itself without motion; it is motion. When we give ourselves over to language, however, what we learn, paradoxically is that we cannot learn precisely all we want about it from itself. Its meaning is distributed through different words, still more language. It does not confer its own meaning; it points us always elsewhere, to things other than itself. Language gives us its meaning by giving us its opacity.

Merleau-Ponty writes: "There is thus an opaqueness of language. Nowhere does it stop and leave a place for pure meaning, it is always limited only by more language, and meaning appears within it only set in a context of words. Like a charade."[19] When we are dealing with language, we are dealing with opacity. Nowhere, he says, does language stop. Opacity, then, is connected to movement, suggesting transparency as a property of stillness. This interplay of movement, meaning, and silence is captured in the simile that follows: like a charade, one individual movement does not mean anything, it is when the whole is taken together that one can arrive at meaning. The metaphors for language, particularly the characterization of its opacity, are visual, and its materialization spatial, in contrast to the auditory metaphors and examples that come later in the essay, including the click of the woman's heel. The example of the charade effectively divorces the realms of the visual and the auditory. In a charade, any auditory information accompanying the gesture means that a charade ceases to be a charade, ceases to be itself. A charade, however, is never really or only itself even when it is itself. It is defined as such only through its embodied mimetic relation to some other action or person, the reenactment of that other action or person thorough embodied gesture. Gesture expresses meaning through expressing style. As Galen Johnson describes it in his essay on Merleau-Ponty's "Indirect Language" titled "Structures and Painting": "Style begins as soon as any person perceives the world, and all perception stylizes because embodiment is a style of the world. Our own living body is a special way of accenting the variants the world offers."[20] The body has a style, expresses a style through movement and gesture, and style can be understood as something other than, and even resistant to, the choice or will of an individual artist, or person, even as it is her or his uniquely embodied expression.

Merleau-Ponty offers walking as a metaphor by which we might understand the relation between meaning and language, the footprint as the fixed trace of a movement that has passed on: "Language ends up imposing the most precise identification upon us in a flash. . . . Language bears the meaning of thought as a footprint signifies the movement and effort of a body."[21] He is interested in the ways in which meaning is transmitted in a flash, suddenly, wholly and entirely. We do not arrive at meaning in a synthetic way, by adding together individual elements. It is given in language suddenly, "in a flash," and also given through gesture with that same suddenness. It is not always possible to see precisely *how* gesture expresses style, not possible to freeze-frame movements, to stop time and try to locate the essence of gesture there. Although sometimes, like the painter who filmed himself painting in order to better learn his own gestures, we need to try.

In the epigraph to this chapter, Judith Butler relates of the story of a young man in Maine who is murdered for his queer walk by boys who "feel that they must negate this person, they must expunge the trace of this person. They must stop that walk no matter what." In that walk, there was clearly a conversation of gestures taking place, though perhaps it was a one way conversation, or one in which the participants were only indirectly engaging one another. It seems that this young man's walk changed over time; as he grew up, its swish became more pronounced, more "dramatically feminine." The gender and sexual significations of his walk became more emphatic and distinct as he got older, and it may have been the intensification of his swish, and not simply the swish itself, that infuriated the other boys and drove them to murderous violence.

In the King case, the click of Latisha's heels down the hallway is understood by the teachers to represent a danger. We can notice the ways in which concern for Latisha's safety are articulated, the shift in focus in how that danger is characterized. The danger is at first named as Latisha herself—she will fall down, she will twist her own ankle, she will break her own neck. This soon morphs into a different concern, related but with a different agent of danger: she will make herself a target. Someone else will break her neck. "Larry" was "sticking himself out," Shirley Brown states, as she assures the court with egalitarian equanimity that she was not singling anyone out, that she would have taken any boy aside who was "sticking himself out," who was making himself a target. In the next chapter, we will explore the function of sticking out and passing, of anonymity and individuation, in the way Latisha was perceived at school.

o o o

One day Latisha wore eye shadow to school, and a teacher, though not one of hers, told her to wash it off. The teacher, Jill Eckman, said that Latisha did so, compliantly, but returned the next day with eye shadow on again, defiantly. "He said he had *rights*" she said, contemptuously. Latisha's "defiance" was often described in terms of gesture. Indeed, in her opening argument, Maeve Fox speaks of Latisha's increasing confidence, and her changing gender presentation, this way: "Some say that his confidence level increased. Larry King started to decide he wasn't going to take it anymore. He started reacting to the teasing and the shoving. He started giving it back, some attitude." At this moment, the district attorney pauses, hesitates, looking for a proper description for this change in Latisha. When linguistic description was not sufficient to the task of characterizing Latisha in the last weeks of her life, the district attorney resorts to enacting Latisha's gestures through her own body. Or, more precisely, she enacts a gesture that she does not attribute to Latisha, but that she understands to in some way encapsulate the style of Latisha's gestural life. Fox bends an arm at the elbow, places her hand under her chin, palm down, then slides it quickly outward, in a kind of inverted salute: the chin flick. She makes this gesture with her hand and arm, and then describes it this way: "He was giving the proverbial chin, or the proverbial f-you." Latisha, as she is described by Fox in this moment (embodying the "fuck you" familiar from the proverbs?), is through some remarkable alchemy able to transform the transphobic scorn directed her way into something powerful and profound, a sense of confidence and security held at a bodily level.

In Fox's account, Latisha is able to mobilize gesture in order to refuse the belittlement of her peers. Or, to be more accurate, Latisha is articulating her life through her comportment, her dress, her movements, and her relations with others *in such a way that her very style of embodiment comes to resemble this gesture*. Merleau-Ponty says of the power of gesture that it can enable the body to exceed itself and its circumstances in the world. He writes: "The body's gesture toward the world introduces it into an order of relations of which pure physiology and biology do not have the least idea. Despite the diversity of its parts, which makes it fragile and vulnerable, the body is capable of gathering itself into a gesture which for a time dominates its dispersion and puts its stamp upon everything it does."[22] Gesture, then, gives us a way of seeing how the body and its meaning are not primarily biological, but rather that they engage and exceed the biological. And it seems a particularly apt way of describing Latisha, both the effect that her gendered style of embodiment had on others, her gestures that seemed to resonate so strongly throughout the school, and the way in which her gestures organized and made coherent her body and her person. The gestures of her gender presentation and her confidence and even defiance in the face of condemnation were how she transcended her fragility and a means by which her diversity of parts—scarred body, slight frame, challenged organs, medicated brain—could coalesce into a unity of proud, fierce, outsized expression.

This fierce expression found its apex in Latisha's walk, brashly gendered, but according to her teachers too misplaced in her male body to qualify as feminine. The fact that her walk was so gendered, or so wrongly gendered, actually removed it from the category of walking. During the testimony of one teacher, Arthur Saenz, Defense Attorney Robyn Bramson and he struggle to find the language to describe Latisha's walk: it was not a walk so much as it was a *parading*, a *parading back and forth*, a *cocking like a bird*. A man sitting behind me in the gallery chimes in during their back-and-forth, volunteering in a stage whisper: *sashaying*. As lawyer and witness continue casting about for language, and finding each word unsatisfactory, the blizzard of gerunds begins to slow, and they start to use their bodies to demonstrate the gender performance for which no words are deemed sufficient. "Was it, was it, what kind of walk was it? Was it like—?" And the defense attorney puts her hand on her hip, thrusts her chin high up in the air, and starts walking back and forth, swinging her hips. Well it was more like: the witness wiggles in his seat, lifts an arm up into the air, then lets his wrist go limp. He performs the gay walk in his chair, she adjusts her walk to match his, and they act out the gay-ness of Latisha's "parading," as they have decided to name it, back and forth across the courtroom, in a duet of mockery. When a style of walking is too queer, it stops being a walk and becomes a *prancing* or a *mincing* or a *cocking* or a *sashay*. It is no longer a walk at all. And the gestural meaning of the exchange between lawyer and witness was perfectly clear, even though that meaning evaded capture by the official court transcript. [23]

The contention in this case was that when Latisha walks down the hallway in her boots, she was making an issue of her gender. She was "throwing it at people," in the words of Dawn Boldrin. That the teachers who police Latisha's gender also have a gender is seemingly invisible to them. But when a teacher herself clicks down the hall, or squishes down it in practical shoes with crepe soles, she, too, is offering her gender to the world, even if it recedes from her attention in its conformation with the norms of gender. Even if her shoes—perfectly appropriate, nearly invisible in their dullness—escape attention. Even if they do not make her a target.

V. AGGRESSION, PROJECTION, HORIZON

A click is a sound that resonates with gendered significance. It is also a sound that can echo with racial significance. Consider this statement: "There are very few African-American men who haven't had the experience of walking across the street and hearing the locks click on the doors of cars." An African-American man is walking down the street and hears a "click," the sound of white fear, of a racist social imaginary. President Obama, who was speaking after the shooting of Trayvon Martin, continued: "That happens to me, at least before I was a senator."[24] Philosopher George Yancy describes a similar moment, a "deafening" hail of clicks, in which he is racialized, marked, entrapped, in a passage that echoes Fanon. In the scene Yancy narrates, the clicks emerge from a white femininity consolidating itself against a blackness that it is consolidating in turn:

> The sounds of car doors locking are deafening: *Click. Click. Click. Click. Click. Click. Click. ClickClickClickClick-ClickClickClick.* The *clicking* sounds are always accompanied by nervous gestures and eyes that want to look but are hesitant to do so. The *click* ensures their safety, effectively re-signifying their white bodies as in need of protection from *blackness*, that site of danger, death, and doom. In fact, the *clicks* begin to return me to myself—even as I continue to disrupt the constituting effects of the clicks that overdetermine me—as a dangerous beast. The *clicks* attempt to seal my identity as a dark savage. The *clicking* sounds mark me; they inscribe me, materializing my presence, as it were, in ways that I know to be untrue.[25]

o o o

In writing about the killing of Trayvon Martin in 2012, Yancy has noted: "To be a black man is to be marked for death." We have seen this repeatedly in recent months and years in the United States, with the shooting of black man after black man after black man by police. Black bodies are caricatured as dangerous and feared, a characterization that is then used to justify the violence against them. We can see, too, the critical significance of gesture in these cases, in which the hands of a black man holding a bag of skittles or a book or nothing at all are fantasized as and thus transformed into hands that threaten by the racist imaginary of the one who actually holds the weapon. In this imaginary, even the universal gesture of *hands up, don't shoot* is enough to get a person of color shot.

Yancy has noted the ways in which, during George Zimmerman's trial for the killing of Martin, "Racial profiling could not be invoked by the prosecution, which meant that the truth about Black bodies and anti-Black racism as expressed through racial technologies could not be told, which meant that the trial, in my view, was a site of obfuscation; a sham. Having the discourse of racial profiling barred by the state implicates the state in denying the use of the necessary narrative that implicates Zimmerman in acts of anti-Black racism and the devaluation of Trayvon Martin's life." Yancy describes the ways in which devaluation and marginalization makes some lives matter more than others, marks the bodies of black men vulnerable as the state targets them with impunity. And then there is the "obfuscation" and "sham" of a legal process that is unwilling to recognize racism, in either its structural or its particular predations.

The fantasy of aggression in the King case is most startling for the ways in which it gains coherence by taking the form of paranoid projection.[26] It is important to attend to the conditions under which a narrative of homophobic or transphobic violence becomes or fails to become coherent, and what different guises aggression can take in such narratives. I would like in this context to think a bit about another King incident, the beating of black motorist Rodney King by the Los Angeles police in 1991. We see in both instances that the actions of violence directed at the vulnerable are made possible through a fantasy structure in which the perpetrators of that violence attribute an aggressivity to those vulnerable subjects. Indeed, such a structure of projected aggressivity is perhaps the only way of explaining how strapping Brandon McInerney could cast the slender and undersized Latisha King as an aggressive threat, or how a gang of heavily armed police officers acting in concert could argue that an inert Rodney King constituted a lethally dangerous threat, even as the mass of them were clubbing his body as it lay motionless on the ground. The fact that the argument was legally successful in the 1991 case, exonerating the police officers, suggests that this fantasy structure is somehow sensical to the law and aligned with cultural expectation, even if it conjures a situation entirely contrary to the manifest physical reality of the scene. I am arguing that the most pernicious forms of violence are able to work, are perhaps *only able to work*, through these fantasies of aggression projected onto a victim. Such projections become the justification for homophobic and racist violence, refiguring the socially enjoined violence visited on vulnerable bodies as a defensive act on the part of the more powerful. There is of course all manner of difference between the operations of racism, homophobia, and transphobia. But the structures that give rise to such socially enjoined violence share features in common. The commonality between Latisha King and Rodney King was even noted by Rodney King himself in his 2012 autobiography *The Riot Within*, in which he compares himself to the other King, the one who did not survive. "The thing I find so frustrating about these front-page stories," Rodney King writes, "is that we're not moving forward as a race of people, towards a more peaceful path of tolerance and understanding. We're just as close-minded and violent as we were twenty years ago when I was brutally beaten and tasered by police. We're just as prejudiced and poisoned by hate as we were when my gay teacher friend Mr. Jones was shot and killed by a vengeful student from John Muir High School. What have we learned? How have we changed? What have we improved?"[27]

In looking at the two King cases together, we see that the aggression attributed to queer or trans subjects and the aggression attributed to black subjects share three temporal attributes. First, the supposed aggression is retroactively installed as temporally prior, a "threat" that can be marked only after the body in question has already been the object of violence. Second, the attribution of aggression then gives the violence leveled at vulnerable subjects the cover story of preemption; that violence is "self-defense" against an aggression that would presumably have taken place sometime in the future. And third is the question of the ontology of that aggression, which, since it is both conjectural and futural, is not materially visible. Conjuring such violence and attributing it to vulnerable subjects and bodies thus relies on strategies of fixing, freezing, or altogether breaking the representational frame in order that the violence that supposedly inheres in the violated body might appear in the fractured reflection that results. In the Latisha King case, that freezing of the representational frame occurred through the invocation, over and over, of Larry King, in school, dressed in feminine clothing. In the Rodney King case, that freezing happened in the trial, when the videotape of the beating was disassembled by the defense into a series of still images, which had the effect of simultaneously mitigating the brutality of the beating he was receiving and rendering him as noncompliant. To be a black man is to be marked with death. What is it, then, to be a black transwoman? How is one's life as a black transwoman marked, as a member of a population still more marked by such fatality?

As a way of thinking these two cases alongside each other, I would like to consider the phenomenological concept of the horizon. This idea, which originated with Husserl and was elaborated by Merleau-Ponty, holds that the world, when considered phenomenologically, is centered in my own perspective but also always shared. I am not the singular author of my meaning or my life, but rather my life and its meaning are best understood as a collaborative project of bodies whose contextual horizons are necessarily shared. The result is a lifeworld that is social, in which the engendering and interpretation of meaning is a relational activity. Horizons are shared because they coexist in enmeshment with one another. This does not mean, however, that they are equal; one of the most helpful things about the concept of a horizon is its ability to describe a world characterized by asymmetrical power relations and the differential distribution of bodily vulnerability that is a consequence of that power asymmetry. As we will see in the last chapter, one might describe the project of ethics as attention to what should happen when horizons are shared, in contradistinction with what often *does* happen when they are. One of the most significant workings of power in the creation of the social world is precisely that power can delegitimize other horizons, can render them as untrue, invisible, or unthinkable. One of power's effects can be to break or dissolve the horizon that makes the other's body, and life, legible, substituting its own horizon in the place of the other's.

An example of just such an unhappy enmeshment of conflicting horizons can be found in the Rodney King beating. The capture and dissection of that beating on videotape, and particularly the subsequent exoneration of the police officers who beat him, offer an example of different horizons, discrepancies that interrupt the presumption or, indeed, the experience of a shared horizon as a unified horizon. In her article on Rodney King, "Endangered/ Endangering," Judith Butler points to the dangers of misrecognizing a reading as a seeing, the kind of misrecognition that in this case facilitated the white Simi Valley jury's acceptance of the police interpretation of the videotape of King's beating. That jury believed the police assertions that King was aggressively threatening the police officers, even as the evidence they were offered showed police beating him aggressively as he offered little resistance.

Gail Weiss takes up Butler's reading to ask if an attempt to counter the racially saturated horizon in which the videotape was viewed with an aggressive antiracist reading, or an "antiracist hegemony," in Butler's terms, does not risk achieving only a further saturation of the horizon with aggression. She writes: "Although Butler's strategy of countering a racist hegemony with an antiracist hegemony may be rhetorically and politically effective, I think it is also extremely problematic. . . . Is aggressivity either necessary or sufficient to promote the viability of alternative readings to the Rodney King incident, and to other equally disturbing events in recent and past U.S history? And if it is, then is there a way of distinguishing the violence and aggressivity deployed in the antiracist reading from the violence and aggressivity that inheres in the racist one?"[28] Weiss asks what grounds might be used to determine the legitimacy of the antiracist reading over the racist one, given that Butler has asserted that seeing is always already interpreting and that therefore there can be no Truth of events that is not already mediated and thus no way to use the event itself, outside of interpretation, for its evidentiary value to support either reading.

I would offer that one way of distinguishing the violence and aggression in the racist reading and the antiracist one is to attend to the target of the aggression. That is to say, Butler advocates an aggressive *reading* of the video and suggests that such a reading should be "repeated and publicized." The aggressive readings that Butler advocates hinges on a different understanding of black men, white police, and the general populace than the interpretation that eventually prevailed in court. The "antiracist hegemony" that Butler hopes to further would appear, in the light of the King verdict (and, indeed, subsequent events in the racial life of Los Angeles), to be a utopic counterpoint to actual conditions, politically necessary to reach toward, but on a quite different ontological plane than, the hegemony that it is seeking to counter.

In comparing these two horizons, the relations of power that currently exist render any attempt to represent them as equivalent a purely formal exercise, not responsive to their actual appearance in the world. Discerning the scope and depth of these horizons is not, then, a matter of squaring them with any kind of pre-representational or pre-interpretive truth, but rather a matter of determining which interpretation seems more attuned to the phenomena it seeks to describe and attending to the effects of each. The effects of an antiracist hegemony might be to expand or resuscitate a collective political imaginary that finds itself injured or splintered by that other horizon, the racist hegemony, whose effects can be seen in the broken body of Rodney King, as well as in the verdict that exonerated the officers who beat him.

Robert Gooding-Williams suggests that it is precisely the everyday violence of systematic racism that was the context for the all-too common instance of police brutality and the vehicle through which the extraordinary verdict was possible.[29] We see in this moment the political necessity of maintaining some conceptual distinction between the body of a text, the body of a reading, and the human body, and note that the task of finding adequate ways to describe the phenomena that one encounters brings political work and phenomenological method into deep accord. Aggression as a reading strategy may work to counter the logics of aggression that determine the visible field and counter the routes of power through which anti-racist and anti-queer violence justifies itself. That such power constitutes the horizons we occupy is also one of the reasons that altering or expanding them is often more difficult than we would like.

That expansion of the horizon is sometimes called a school. The school as institution was once described in the following way, as a place that succeeds to the extent that it widens the horizon of its students:

> A secondary school should achieve more than not driving its pupils to suicide. It should give them a desire to live and should offer them support and backing at a time of life at which the conditions of their development compel them to relax their ties with their parental home and their family. It seems to me indisputable that schools fail in this, and in many respects fall short of their duty of providing a substitute for the family and of arousing interest in life in the world outside.[30]

This is from Freud's "Contributions to a Discussion on Suicide," written about a hundred years ago. It is a sober assessment of the failure of schools to address suicidal despair in students, and provides an account of the purpose of schools and of education that is almost exactly contrary to the common understanding of the educational imperative as one of cloister and shelter. Freud suggests that protection should not be the model of a school, and shelter from the world is not the aim of an education. In the moment that a young person is beginning to find modes of relation outside the family, Freud says, the school must provide a substitute. But the substitute for the family is not structured like a family. Arguably the greatest value of a school is its ability to become an elsewhere, to give us models that are precisely not the family model, ones that offer us a different structure through which to feel and disseminate affection, intimacy, and aggression. The most important task of a school, Freud says, is to awaken desire. Protection, in such a context, would function only as an increasing fortification, an ever-narrowing constriction of sociality collapsing in on itself. He proposes, then, a pedagogical erotics that encourages the student to take the outside world, and the life found there, as an object of desire, even at the expense of his or her attachment to the school itself. For it is not any life, or even proximate life, that the student needs to desire, but the life found in the world outside: "The school must not take on itself the inexorable character of life: it must not seek to be more than a *game* of life."[31]

VI. SUICIDE

For a number of years, I have had Eve Sedgwick's essay "Queer and Now" as the first item on my Queer Theory syllabus, a text that we consider collectively, as a class, on the first day of our meeting. It begins as follows: "I think everyone who does gay and lesbian studies is haunted by the suicides of adolescents. To us, the hard statistics come easily: that queer teenagers are two to three times likelier to attempt suicide, and to accomplish it, than others; that up to 30 percent of teen suicides are likely to be gay."[32] Sedgwick wrote these lines in 1993, and it is hard to know which is more startling: that these observations about youth suicide still have the immediacy that they do, or that queer suicides have only now become news. Sedgwick's introduction can easily stand as a contemporary assessment of our current moment, perhaps adding only trans energies and lives alongside the queer, acknowledging that their bodies and selves are still more vulnerable than gay youth. In the next sentence, Sedgwick's describes the kind of knowledge that we have about these suicides and confirms something about their epistemological ambiguity: "The knowledge is indelible, but not astonishing, to anyone with a reason to be attuned to the profligate way this culture has of denying and despoiling queer energies and lives. I look at my adult friends and colleagues doing lesbian and gay work, and I feel that the survival of each one is a miracle. Everyone who survived has stories about how it was done." If this knowledge is indelible, its ineradicable traces are inscribed on a surface or in a location that is itself perpetually at risk of being lost.

A pessimistic reading of the fresh surprise at each decade's wave of queer suicides might understand it as a confirmation that the conditions under which such suicides occur are both intractable and occluded, perhaps systemically so. How best to address the despair behind such suicides? As Sedgwick poses the question: "How to tell kids who are supposed never to learn this that, farther along, the road widens and the air brightens; that in the big world there are worlds where it's plausible, our demand to *get used to it.*"[33] That phrase *get used to it* cannot ring in the ears of contemporary youth with the same resonance that it did in 1993, where it was a demand that straight culture acknowledge the presence of queer lives. Yet Sedgwick's question about how to communicate that more open horizon to dispirited and imperiled queer youth describes the same sentiment that impels Dan Savage's "It Gets Better" YouTube campaign addressing queer youth at risk of suicide: the road widens, the air brightens, *it gets better.*

In 2010, in between the time of the murder and the murder trial, Dan Savage launched the "It Gets Better" campaign in an attempt to reach out to despairing and suicidal LGBT youth to try and convince them that despite the direness of their current circumstances, life does indeed get better for LGBT people. The campaign was justly criticized on a number of fronts: for being too simplistic, for universalizing the perspective of the white gay male with class privilege, for suggesting the inevitability of upward mobility.[34] It is surely true that life does not get better for all of us. It is true that we do not all survive. I am most interested in the critique that the campaign is relentlessly future-focused instead of being concerned with the present, anticipating a later time when conditions will surely improve and advocating a strategy of waiting out the present day rather than changing things now. That last critique, along with a critique of the portrayal of queer youth as martyrs or victims, is a rather uncanny replication of Lee Edelman's position in *No Future*, a book that has been a widely criticized and an immensely generative counterpoint in recent queer theory. Indeed, one of the things that José Esteban Muñoz invited us to take seriously in his critique of Edelman in *Cruising Utopia* is the proposition that *the future matters*, that leaning toward a utopian future that can be imagined even if it cannot yet be materially realized can be an engagement with politics and not simply a flight from politics. Hope is sometimes necessarily predicated on an incipient future that exceeds the grasp of the pragmatic, and queer practices of art-making and world-making are sometimes the best ways to lean toward that future.

Part of what has been criticized in this campaign is its passivity. Some suggest that it ought to emphasize the power of the individual to change his or her own circumstances: thus *make it better* instead of *it gets better*. The slogan of "make it better" affirms will as the proper rubric for understanding both the triumphs and failures of queer life. The thing that might give us pause about that last criticism is its invocation of an agentic individual who is able to effectively mobilize power to make his or her circumstances better, as a corrective to the more collectivist and contextual horizon of the more nebulous "it" that either gets better, or doesn't, aside from the purposefully instrumentalized will of the youth suffering the fact that it is not better yet.

In short, what one might need in that moment is a shared horizon. Viewing the world in terms of shared horizons suggests that a change to the conditions of my life can result only from something other than my own causally efficacious actions. It seems to me that aspects of Sedgwick's queer approach, or perhaps a queer approach in general, is that it teaches us to look at structures rather than individual actors when considering both the causes and the solutions to violence against queers and transpeople. How then, in this context, should we begin to reckon with these disturbing suicides, which are more chilling not because they represent a new development, but exactly because they are the norm, exactly because they are perfectly in line with what we have known about LGBT suicide for decades. What might unite violence against LGBT youth that comes in the form of murder and violence that comes in the form of suicide? What might Freud's comments on suicide, and his characterization of suicide as a murder of the self, contribute to these issues? I was initially hesitant to use Freud's comments to read these instances of LGBT suicide. Understanding suicide as self-murder seemed to me to risk replicating the individualist analytic of above, to replace an analysis of the social contexts that push the vulnerable toward suicide by locating the aggression within the suicidal person, in a projection of aggressive violence that is all too common where queer folks are concerned, as we have seen. This same individualist analytic would have it that Brandon McInerney was merely a bad seed, that the killing was a result of an individual evil person, thus obscuring the role played by the school, the parents, the teachers—and shrinking the field of responsibility down to one fourteen-year-old boy.

The terrible economy of suicide lies in the simultaneity of its inward and outward action, that this kind of punishment is a routing of aggression that cannot find a direction outward and so turns back in on the self, while still retaining its function as an aggression toward the other. Jacqueline Rose has described this same dual movement of suicide less in terms of inner topography and more in terms of the social conditions under which it occurs:

> All suicides kill other people. However isolated the moment, suicide is also always an act of cruelty. . . . Suicide is rarely the singular, definitive act it appears to be. The ego, Freud tells us, turns onto itself the hatred it feels towards

the object. But the object is never spared. No one commits suicide, psychoanalyst Karl Menninger wrote, unless they experience at once 'the wish to die, the wish to kill, the wish to be killed'. You can die, but you can't commit suicide, on your own.[35]

Despite the isolation, both perceived and real, of those queer youth who violently end their own lives, their deaths extend outward: "You can die, but you can't commit suicide on your own." The responses to these deaths, the addresses to anonymous others and the insistence that it gets better is not merely a well-meaning platitude spouted by anxious adults who have safely steered their lives into a harbor of privilege, but an invitation into a different future that is unknown. A shared horizon, in this instance, cannot indicate spatial or temporal proximity or even community. That is, in the invocation of "it gets better," I wonder if there is not something in the vagueness of that "it"—the passive voice, nonagentic, nonindexical—that might be thought of as precisely the location of that hope? If I am a trans or queer youth who feels at the end of my rope, with no resources and nowhere to turn, the very thing that might sustain me in that moment is that there is an *it* that can get better exactly when I have reached the limit of my own capacity to make anything at all improve, even without specifying its contours of features. In that way the abstractness of the world invoked, its distance from what I can know or imagine in this moment and also from my own will, allows my own horizon to widen and to offer a way to an outside, to the as-yet unknown, to a differently valenced life.

But sometimes, it does not get better. Sometimes pointing toward some sunnier future horizon is not enough.

Sometimes it gets worse. Sometimes it ends. The last time I taught Queer Theory, I began the first day of the semester as I always do, with a collective consideration of "Queer and Now." We sat with Sedgwick's haunted contemplation of the suicides of queer adolescents. We were a small seminar that year, just a handful of students. Most of them queer. Half students of color. One of them did not survive to the end of the term. Suicide.

○ ○ ○

One of the most remarkable things about Latisha King's short life was her resilience, the way that she persevered in her self-expression in the face of normative regulation and prohibition. She emerged, and persisted, in defiance of all the different forms of violence directed at her, with the aim of extinguishing her very being. She was not crushed into submission by the insistence, by family and teachers and peers, that she was impossible, that she did not exist—though all these forms of violence did exact their price. On the morning that she was shot, she had dressed herself in compliance with the school's dress code. On that day, she wore her boy drag. That day, she was passing as Larry. And yet, dressed in boy's clothes, sitting in her classroom, she typed her name: *Latisha King*. These were the first words on the computer screen, the first two words of her essay, the essay that according to her teacher's recollection consisted at that point of nothing other than those first two words: her name. She had given herself a name, and she wrote it out, so that everyone huddled around her computer screen, some laughing, some pointing, some with hands covering their mouths, could see. *Latisha King. I am here.*

3

ANONYMITY

I. EVERYONE AND NO ONE,
OR THE PARADOX OF PHENOMENOLOGY

Thus far in this book I have leaned into the resources offered by phenomenology in order to read and analyze the ways in which gender and sexuality, as embodied phenomena, were enacted in the school and brought into the courtroom. But how might we think beyond the level of individuated bodies to consider the body of the school as a whole and its role in the case? I will suggest that phenomenology can also offer us a way to read the gestalt of the world in which this murder occurred, the social context in which Brandon and Latisha were and were not held, together and apart. In what follows, I trace the concept of anonymity in phenomenology to read the climate and conditions of the relational world of the school, and suggest that it can help illuminate some of the paradoxes of Latisha's place, and displacement, in the school environment. Anonymity in this sense names the realm that was denied Latisha through surveillance of her gender. And "common sense," its epistemological corollary, was the means by which a consensus was reached between teachers and students about Latisha's gender as a dangerous weapon. Anonymity becomes the cover for normative violence, as it was when Brandon suggested during the trial that he thought he was "doing everyone a favor" by shooting Latisha, because "everyone hated him," because "no one liked him." The key to understanding the social force that gathered momentum behind these invocations of *everyone* and *no one* can be found in this particular variant of anonymity.

Merleau-Ponty has been described by at least one commentator as a philosopher of anonymity, simply by virtue of the fact that compared to his more celebrated contemporaries, he is less well known. "In many respects," writes Jack Reynolds, "Merleau-Ponty is the unknown man of the twentieth century's major European philosophers."[1] Which is not to say that he has not been tremendously influential; rather, as Reynolds argues, it is "simply to observe that his life and personality have not been examined." In a way it is perfectly fitting that Merleau-Ponty should be thought of as not just a philosopher of anonymity, but an anonymous philosopher in the routine sense of that word. Anonymity has one meaning when used in a common everyday sense, and another, or several others, when used in a phenomenological sense. And like a number of other phenomenological terms–"intention" and "flesh" are two other examples of concepts that are related but not reducible to their commonplace counterparts—the phenomenological concept of anonymity shares meaning with the way the term is normally used, but also adds to and departs from it. Anonymity, in the sense that we routinely deploy it, connotes an unknown-ness, an absence or an evacuation of a proper name.[2] Anonymity in its phenomenological sense also evokes this meaning, but shifts its emphasis. Anonymous life refers not to what is missing—a proper name, a mode of being consolidated under the sign of individuated personhood—but to that mode of life that exists and persists in the absence of those principles of organization and containment. As we shall see, such a mode of life can be a way of inhabiting my connection with others that subtends or transcends individuated personhood.

A foray, then, into the relationship between anonymity and phenomenology. As a branch of philosophy, phenomenology is concerned with the transcendent structures of consciousness, the shared, invariant, and "universal" features of experience that all consciousnesses share. This is the way that Husserl characterizes phenomenology, calling it an "eidetic science," the rigorous and systematic inquiry into essences. However, phenomenology also names that area of philosophy that focuses on the perspectively specific nature of experience, the particularity of the world that I and I alone inhabit, even simply by virtue of the uniqueness of my location in time and space. This can be understood as a tension between phenomenology considered in its strict Husserlian sense and phenomenology as it came to be articulated in the social sciences in the mid-twentieth century. But one need not delineate a distinction between classical or transcendental phenomenology and "applied" phenomenology, or phenomenology as it came to merge through and as psychology and the social sciences, to find such a tension. This tension need not even be understood as problematic, and can be discerned at the very advent of phenomenology in the work of Husserl. It would surely be an error to try to render phenomenology, or any branch of philosophy, free of contradiction or even to require of it a coherence that it may not possess, particularly at its most nascent stage. As Dorion Cairns puts it, "By phenomenology Husserl meant whatever he was doing at the time."[3] Take, for instance, the relation between the aim and the means of what may be his most foundational contribution to phenomenological method, the phenomenological reduction. The aim of the phenomenologist is to arrive to the world, to know it as it is, to allow her faith in it. And the means by which she arrives at that faith is by rigorously abstaining from her belief in it, holding herself apart from it, subjecting it to a dispassionate scrutiny in which she withholds her judgment concerning it. While the phenomenological reduction as method was largely left behind by Heidegger and Merleau-Ponty, Husserl's most significant descendants, its germ contains this antipathetic structure, a coming to consciousness of the nature of the world through rigidly holding myself outside of the "natural attitude," the mode through which I move through the world in its everydayness, unreflectively.

This tension that is central to phenomenology might better be called an ambiguity rather than a paradox. One of phenomenology's critical insights is that all of human experience is characterized by a fundamental ambiguity. Its significance cannot be resolved into one determined and self-evident meaning. It is always something, and also always inescapably this other thing, and it can never be perceived as both of those things at one and the same moment, even though it must needs contain them both within its horizon. Simone de Beauvoir will take this insight as foundational for ethics.[4] Merleau-Ponty will see in ambiguity a way of explicating the nature of bodily being—my body as always what comprises me as a subject, and also what constitutes me as an object for other people.[5]

Another of Husserl's students extended his legacy in a somewhat different direction. Alfred Schütz worked at the intersection of phenomenological philosophy and social science. Maurice Natanson describes Schütz as performing a phenomenology of the social world "*within* the natural attitude."[6] These—the emphasis on transcendental structures and the emphasis on the lived world, the social world—do not cancel each other out. Indeed, they *cannot*, according to Schütz; as Natanson observes: "A constitutive phenomenology of the natural attitude—even one carried out within the natural attitude—is an interpretive demarcation of the estate of phenomenology, not a repudiation of the results of transcendental reduction."[7]

A phenomenology of the natural attitude would seem to be a different kind of phenomenology than what Husserl proposes, and it is not entirely clear how such reflexive analytical work could be carried out *within* the natural attitude. But this "demarcation of the estate of phenomenology" turns out to also be its work, and we get a clear indication of this from the major philosophical works by Merleau-Ponty (*Phenomenology of Perception*), Schütz (*The Phenomenology of the Social World*), Heidegger (*Introduction to Phenomenological Research*), and Husserl (pretty much everything), each of which not only begins by asking the question "What is phenomenology?" but keeps at it, asking the question over and over again. In that reflexive move, phenomenology becomes again something other than, something opposed to, the natural attitude, even as the natural attitude is its unfading concern. I would like to draw on the first two of these thinkers to suggest that their concepts of anonymity might serve as a place where phenomenology can be thought simultaneously as both inquiry into transcendental essences and also a means of explicating individuation and particularity.

II. OTHERNESS AND COMMON SENSE

We might think of the concept of anonymity as one way that these two aspects of phenomenology, which we can for the sake of clarity refer to as the "transcendentalist thesis" and the "perspectival thesis," might be reconciled or bridged. Anonymity, I will suggest, is one place in which articulated points of their overlap and connection become visible. In his monograph on Alfred Schütz, titled *Anonymity*, Maurice Natanson identifies anonymity as a fundamental theme for Schütz, who sets it next to two other terms, *otherness* and *common sense*. Common sense names the way in which knowledge is held and transmitted within an anonymous mode, knowledge that everyone has. It is collective and shared and seemingly untroubled by internal contradiction or division. When consulted, common sense speaks with one voice. Common sense promises to resolve rather than generate contradiction.

As it is commonly described, common sense seems also to name a way of figuring things out, an epistemological method, and not just a shared repository of information. As Leonard Lawlor puts it, "We know we are in the realm of common sense when somebody says 'everybody knows.'"[8] Common sense is distinguished from what Schütz refers to elsewhere as a "reserve stock of knowledge."[9] If someone exhorts me: "Use your common sense!" that person is generally not suggesting that I already possess the information I need to resolve the problem at hand, but that in possessing common sense I possess the means to arrive at that information that I do not yet have, but that I can *derive* through the use of that sense. This would seem to figure common sense as a faculty for which we have a universal capacity. However, the very invocation of common sense itself indicates the reverse. That the call to common sense takes the form of an adjuration points to its absence; one has to be urged to it or recalled toward it only if one is not utilizing it at the time. That it can be said of someone "she has no common sense" already uncouples the idea of the common from the idea of the universal.

But the context of the call for common sense also bears examining. It emerges most often at the moment in which common sense appears to have already to have failed. That is, the appeal to common sense emerges exactly and only in the moment when it is thought to have already been violated. As Natanson describes it, "It is when things go wrong that common sense stirs."[10] When that moment emerges, we are thinking in some way otherwise to common sense. As we saw earlier, an experience of shock enacts a break with common sense. But common sense is not merely a neutral ground that is disrupted by shock. Common sense can also emerge with normative force in response to a shock. It is that which disciplines the otherwise, brings it back when it has strayed from a collectively agreed upon course of deliberation or action. Common sense and shock thus work in concert, either for the purpose of establishing and enforcing norms or with the aim of challenging them.

When things go wrong, we are in the province of otherness. Otherness is, in Natanson's words, "fugitive to common sense."[11] Which is not to say that it is unrelated to common sense, but rather that it demarcates the outer border of common sense—or in the inverted form, that common sense is simply the inside lining of otherness. Natanson prefers the inversion, defining otherness this way: "Otherness is common sense stripped not only of the possibility of being 'otherwise,' but negated in what it is."[12] Otherness, then, is comprised through and composed of common sense, which has assumed its form through being "stripped" of its possibility to assume any different form. It is otherness that has, in effect, sedimented.

There is something of a logical knot here. Schütz says that otherness is "the primordial meaning of anonymity."[13] If common sense is comprised through and composed of anonymity, and otherness is another name for anonymity, its "primordial meaning," then transitivity would suggest a congruence or alliance between common sense and otherness. But if otherness is *at the same time* fugitive to common sense, if common sense is, as Schütz has asserted, the precipitate left when knowledge refuses to engage with otherness, then the relation of these three terms is less than clear.

How, then, ought we think the relation between common sense and the philosophical enterprise? Insofar as they describe opposed approaches to knowing, and to time, we could think of common sense as the enemy of phenomenology; common sense is what we are already supposed to know. The phenomenological method wants to be a means by which we see the world as it really is by consciously holding it in abeyance and shedding ourselves of those things that we already know. This is the only means by which we are able to break out of the world as pre-interpreted, with its meanings already served and digested. To be a perpetual beginner, as Merleau-Ponty and Husserl say we must be if we are to practice phenomenology, is to teach oneself how *not* to rely on common sense, how not to become captured by the fixed categories of what we all already know.

There is, however, nothing resembling a consensus on the scope or value of common sense, nor on its relationship to the phenomenological enterprise. In *The Way of Phenomenology*, Richard Zaner suggests that common sense is not precisely a social consensus about the world, but rather the comparatively thinner fact that there is a world at all. We can each say of this world that it is always inhabited by more people than just myself, and that it is perceptible to my senses. Common sense gives me the world as *sensed in common* with other perceiving subjects. "Common sense life," as he uses the phrase, means the natural attitude. Zaner takes issue with Natanson, and also Schütz, on the matter of common sense life. Whereas Natanson and Schütz, following Husserl, insist that a break with the natural world occurs when we submit it to a process of reflection, of reflexive awareness, Zaner insists that life itself offers us ample opportunity for such moments of break, through tiny mundane encounters or interactions that surprise or shock us out of our habitual engagement with the world. We have seen in chapter 2 the ways in which a shock in the flow of everyday life can resonate, ripple outward, cause a break in unreflective everyday life, a break whose results can be unpredictable. What Zaner is after, however, is something relatively more minor and less consequential. He describes strolling down a crowded urban sidewalk during the holiday season, immersed in thoughts about shopping, gifts, and plans for the season, and suddenly coming face to face with another similarly immersed shopper, right in his path, nearly running into that person. One walker steps aside, out of the way of the other with whom he is suddenly confronted, and the other steps in the same direction at the same moment. He steps aside again, is again unintentionally mirrored by his mirroring other, and the two of them perform a dance impeding one another's way even as they are trying to remove themselves from each other's path. It is in that moment, of confronting the other in a way that breaks me out of my automatic movement toward my goal, that I experience a minor break with the everydayness of my life.

In the sidewalk do-si-do that Zaner describes, a process of "disengagement occurs, however minimally or momentarily" from the seamless flow of everyday life *within the process of daily life itself.* He explains that this enacts "a kind of release from the deep moorings of the general thesis of the natural attitude" and that this occurs without any consciously mobilized reflection, without my effort to transcend the natural attitude.[14] Such a break occurs always in the passive voice. The point, for Zaner, is for us to model our metaphysical musings on those small moments in the daily world, those moments of interruption, rather than needing to retreat to a separate realm suspended above daily life.

Anonymity is neither a state to be aimed toward nor something to be rectified. It is "neither authentic nor inauthentic," writes Schütz, steering our interpretation away from either a Heideggerian or a moralistic slant. It is instead "a necessary condition for there being a social world."[15] It is the fabric from which daily life is woven, the atmosphere of our relations with others and with the world. Aside from his disagreement about the emergence and location of a shock that leads to a disengagement with the "common sense life," Zaner does agree with Natanson and Schütz in his assessment of the task of the phenomenological philosopher. Like anonymity, the natural attitude is not something to be affirmed or denied. Daily life is rather something to be more precisely described and thus disclosed more fully, even as the work of phenomenology neither begins nor ends with that description. He writes:

> As Husserl emphasizes, while the constant affirming of "reality" is the texture of our daily lives, the denial of it is itself but *another thesis* or supposition, one which affirms

the non-being of that reality. That is, unlike Descartes' attempt at universal doubt, the phenomenological philosopher is interested neither in affirming nor in denying anything, but in exploring, or, as I shall want to say later, in *making explicit* what has hitherto been *implicit*.[16]

I will return to this matter below, in looking at a specific appeal to common sense, in order to consider not only how the implicit can be made explicit, but also the social utility of both, and what concealment is able to achieve.

III. "LAWRENCE KING, A HUMAN BEING"

In a murder trial, the charges against the defendant are read out loud in court. In this murder trial, Brandon McInerney is accused of killing Larry King. He is charged with acting with "malice aforethought" to accomplish willful, premeditated murder. When read aloud, the charge sounds like this:

Brandon McInerney is charged with killing Lawrence King, a human being.

The law concerns itself with Brandon McInerney and also with Lawrence King. The first thing that the court wants us to know about the victim is that he is a human being. The life that was killed has to be a human life in order that the killing be considered a homicide; thus the establishment of Lawrence's humanness is one of the first statements uttered in the courtroom. This serves to identify him in some minimal way and will lay the groundwork for the prosecution's claim that the homicide that occurred was a murder, through the syllogistic precision of the criminal code. Murder is the premeditated killing of a human being. Lawrence King was a human being. Brandon McInerney killed Lawrence King with malice aforethought. Therefore, the premeditated killing of Larry King was a murder.

To have one's grievance taken up by the law in this way is at some level to have one's proper name effaced, where "Lawrence King" is the position that becomes occupied by "The People" in *The People vs. Brandon McInerney*. The People, in turn, are a way of naming the prosecution. But it is also to have one's personhood elaborated, simultaneously. The clerk who reads the charges aloud also tells us that the victim is "Larry King, a person." That slight modification, that slight elaboration of the category of "human," offers him as something more specific than a member of the general class of human. He was a person, individuated, living the specificity of a singular life. His humanness is understood to be inflected with, rather than comprised by, attributes of his personhood. Larry's other name, his improper name, Latisha, had only the briefest flicker of life in the school, just those few minutes between the second it was typed on the screen and the second it joined the proper name, Larry, in naming someone who no longer existed.

Latisha's gender, sexuality, and race are obscurely present in the courtroom, invoked either in order to be made explicit, in the case of gender, or to be dismissed, in the case of race. Chapter 1 showed some of the bizarre effects that result from understanding these aspects as separable from personhood, as in the pretrial hearing that determined that race played no part in the case and thereby insured almost no mention of race during the trial even though Latisha King was biracial and Brandon McInerney was charged with belonging to a racist neo-Nazi gang. The district attorney contended that this killing was a hate crime, which means that it was motivated by bias against a particular group of people who share a marker of identity and that bias served as a "substantial motivating factor" in the killing. It was alleged that a gender bias motivated Brandon to kill Latisha. Gender takes many forms in this case. It is a catalyst, it is a provocation. It is a performance, it is an essence. It is protected expression, it is criminal. But for the district attorney's purposes, it meant one thing. In her opening statement, she explained how we ought to understand gender in this case: "Gender here means sex." Given the premise that gender is the same as sex, the jury was from the outset poorly equipped to understand "Larry King" or "his" gender, since "his" sex was never in doubt, even as her gender presentation was emphatically feminine. As Larry King was described in court, his sex was male, as were his pronouns and proper name. Yet through dress, self-naming, naming requests to others, and behavior, it was clear—although never admitted by the court— that Latisha's gender was *girl*. The assertion that gender is sex collapses these categories and gives sex dominion over gender. While we might long for a more sophisticated account of gender here that might be awake to the nuances of gender as it is lived, there are also ways in which this account is telegraphing something more complex than it might at first appear. For even though gender is asserted to be sex, and thus sex is offered as the reason for the bias, we are given no account of bodily morphology, no recitation of anatomy as evidence of "Larry's" sex. His sex is a matter of the clothing that he wears: it is either altered or determined by that clothing. It is thus also a matter of his choosing and donning clothing—an inadvertently performative account of gender in which gender is the effect of the clothing that one puts on.

Or the accessories one wears. Latisha's ostensible "cross dressing," as it was repeatedly termed in the local newspaper, would be more accurately characterized as cross-accessorizing, a phrase that Ken Corbett has used to describe Latisha's appearance. What District Attorney Fox claimed regarding Larry's wearing of feminine boots, jewelry, and hair product, the behaviors for which he was targeted and killed, was that the wearing of the accessories was a pushback against gender-based harassment. Because of the fact that the donning of the accessories was done with pride, the District Attorney was in fact asserting that Latisha was expressing emotional health, rather than emotional distress, in her wearing of women's accessories. The authoring of gender through the donning of accessories was a claim, a declaration, a prideful response to the taunting she received at school. With this claim, both the District Attorney and Latisha captured something real about the assertion of gender expression as a mode of defense. The risk in such a claim, however, is that it relocates Latisha's performance of gender, figuring it as something pushing toward the other, a something that is not defensive, but is in fact aggressive.

And yet, there is some temporal ripple in this account. The teasing is said to have occurred as a result of the gender transgression visible in the dress, but the dressing as a visible expression of gender transgression was ostensibly undertaken to push back against that very harassment. When gender is understood as *something that I do to someone else*, as well as an element of my personhood that expresses itself, the time and the aim of its expression multiply in this way.

This testifies, too, to the unlocatability of gender; a violation of gender norms was apparent in Latisha's person, even before there was any cross-accessorizing, even in the absence of any singular object to which one might have pointed as its location. As we shall see below, anonymity, in both its common and phenomenological usage, depends on compliance with gender norms. This question of Latisha's gender, how and when it asserted itself, and whether it did so in a mode of compliance or defiance, is inextricable from the ways in which she was unable to retreat into anonymity and thus unable to inhabit the shared and reciprocal life of those around her.

Susan Crowley was one of Latisha's teachers who testified to their relationship, to Latisha's behavior, and to her own interventions. She described that relationship while she was being questioned by defense attorney Robyn Bramson:

BRAMSON: Did you have a student named Larry King?

CROWLEY: Yes

BRAMSON: Did you get to know him well?

CROWLEY: Yes.

BRAMSON: You had a good rapport with him.

CROWLEY: Yes. He was very endearing.

BRAMSON: Do you think he liked you?

CROWLEY: Yes. Not initially because I had high expectations but eventually he was fond of me also.

BRAMSON: Over the course of the year did you get a good sense of his personality?

CROWLEY: Yes. [I saw him] twice a day. And he stopped in to see me most days to say hi.

BRAMSON: In seventh grade how would you describe him?

CROWLEY: He got along much better with adults than
he did with kids. He had a small circle of friends [who
were] girls. He liked adult company, liked the attention. He was effeminate and had a high-pitched voice.
He made a present for my cat at Christmas because he
knew I had a cat.

BRAMSON: Did Larry have any behavioral problems?

CROWLEY: He was constantly seeking attention. He was
very endearing but very needy. Much more emotion-
ally immature than other kids his age. He constantly
sought attention.

BRAMSON: And I think you said he was immature?

CROWLEY: He wanted attention but did not have the
social skills to get it. He talked about subjects that
did not. . . . Apropos of nothing he said he had been
crocheting scarves for soldiers in the Middle East. All
the kids caught my eye but then they looked down
and did not say anything because they knew they
could not say anything about him in my classroom.
So afterwards I asked him: Honey what was that
about? Who taught you to crochet? And he said:
My grandma. I said: Do you know anyone else that
crochets? You tell me every day that the other kids
tease you and harass you. But you talk about things
to get attention. That behavior needs to stop. There is
nothing wrong with crochet, but other kids don't do
it. I said that Rosie Greer did cross-stitch but he was
a pro football player and he could get away with it.
This is junior high not junior college and this is not
the time. This is not.

It is apparent that Crowley understands Latisha to have
been fond of her. Latisha came to say hello to her most

days, made a Christmas present for her cat, and sought Crowley's counsel. Crowley also describes Latisha as less mature than her peers, and engaging in behaviors that other kids did not. Here, though, the description turns somewhat strangely on the question of Latisha's maturity. The characterization of her as immature sits alongside the assertions that she got along better with adults than with kids her own age, that the time for her "behavior"—still unspecified—is junior college and not junior high school. She is thus immature, delayed, too early, at the same time that she is too mature, too far ahead, too enmeshed in something—a way of speaking? a way of being? a way of presenting?—that should more properly emerge in "junior college." Latisha's strangeness, her wrongness, becomes a temporal problem as well as a gender problem. Or a temporal problem because the unfolding of gender is a temporal matter.[17]

The suggestion that Latisha is seeking attention comes in this instance from her remark about crocheting. The remark comes "apropos of nothing," Crowley suggests. It marks her as out of sync with her peers, because "the other kids don't do it." The behavior about which she is concerned is not merely the crocheting, but that Latisha is marking herself with the remark, exposing herself in a way that she would not have had she announced that she had been at Jiu Jitsu, as Brandon often was after school, or playing football. Indeed, something like football-playing might have inoculated Latisha, Crowley suggests, allowed her to "get away with" the crochet, just as Rosie Greer got away with the cross-stitch. She recalls what Latisha has confided in her: daily teasing, constant harassment. And her response, given it seems with all attempt at care, is: stop. Stop saying strange things. Quit being weird.

Stop drawing attention to yourself. She was concerned, as so many of the teachers were, with Latisha's "negative attention-seeking," a pseudoclinical turn of phrase that might be translated here as *you are asking for it.*

Crowley understands herself to be Latisha's ally, someone who will take her aside "afterwards," after there has been some incident, after something has gone awry, and intervene. She is looking out for Latisha with these interventions. And also creating a place of protection and maintaining her classroom as a sphere of correct behavior, one in which her other students "knew they could not say anything about him." When Latisha says something odd, a precisely choreographed and wordless dialogue takes place. "All the kids caught my eye," says Crowley: the classroom apparently united as one in their reaction to Latisha's utterance. But there is also an exchange in which the unspoken rule of Mrs. Crowley's classroom is reasserted, the unspoken rule that dictates that you do not speak about Latisha, particularly when she speaks. Latisha speaks, and all of the students "looked down and did not say anything."

In this moment it is all of the other students in the classroom save Latisha who catch Mrs. Crowley's eye. But there are moments when it is Latisha who catches her eye, not with her own look but with how she looks. And when either Latisha or the students who do not know how to respond to her catch Mrs. Crowley's eye, she waits, she lets the moment pass, and she takes Latisha aside after class. She lets Latisha know afterwards, giving her the information she understands her not to have, that she is not participating in the life of the classroom in the proper way, that she is not fitting in, not blending in. Mrs. Crowley begins to give Latisha lessons on how to be anonymous.

IV. SEDIMENTATION AND BASAL ANONYMITY

In Schütz's view, the process through which otherness transforms into common sense is the process of sedimentation. Other transformations are also characterized by the process of sedimentation, namely the acquisition of knowledge, skills, and habits. What Schütz means by "sedimentation" is the way that daily life comes to us pre-interpreted, predigested. With that assessment of daily life as already interpreted, he is describing something like the natural attitude. Sedimentation describes that substratum of knowledge that we have and rely on but cannot quite remember when or how we learned it. We seem always to have known it. He gives the example of a stop sign, or a red light. We know that red means stop, but we can almost never recall when we first learned this, or how. Anonymity is both the means by which we learn much of what we know and also the state that emerges as a result of that learning. Merleau-Ponty, on the other hand, means something quite different with his use of the term sedimentation. For Schütz, sedimentation describes our encounters with the already meaningful shape of the world; sedimentation describes the world. Whereas for Merleau-Ponty, sedimentation describes the means by which I come to be an embodied subject; sedimentation describes me as my habits and body are shaped by and dissolved into the world. For Schütz the antonym of anonymity is *concreteness*. This may strike us as surprising, that anonymity should be contrasted to what is concrete and thus figured as abstract, rather than being contrasted with knowability, or specificity. In Merleau-Ponty, on the other hand, its antonym is something more like "individuated."

Anonymous life is the bodily self I have before there is a "me" to have one.

Merleau-Ponty explains the concept of anonymity in several different ways in *Phenomenology of Perception*. In the chapter titled "The Body in Its Sexual Being," he describes anonymous life as a blank field to which I can retreat when "normal" life, my life lived in connection with others and in co-implication with the world, threatens to capsize me. The later section in the book in which he discusses anonymity at length, "Other Selves and the Human World," is a direct continuation of the discussion of the body in the earlier chapter on sexual being, which concerns anonymity and its relation to natural time, as well as proximity to and withdrawal from the social world. As we shall see, the difference between anonymity as it is articulated in the section on sexual being and the later section is that the former gives us anonymity as a way to retreat from others and the overwhelming press of the social world.[18] The latter gives us anonymity as a way of giving us the other, anonymity as the tissue that forms a continuity out of my body and self and the body and self of the other. Interestingly enough, anonymity here will operate similarly to "flesh" in the later work, as an elemental structure of dual and reversible action.

○ ○ ○

"Other Selves and the Human World" offers prenatal life as exemplary of anonymous life. It is "merely the extreme form," he says, "of that temporal dispersal which constantly threatens the historical present."[19] Of neonatal life, he writes that "nothing was perceived, and therefore there is nothing to recall." This is life that persists, but does not know itself, is not awake to itself. Anonymous life in this articulation is a description of the barest conditions of existence. Things become more complicated, though, as Merleau-Ponty explains that it is not just people who have anonymous life but objects as well. What that ends up meaning is that unlike the thing in the natural world, the subject of the prior chapter, humanly wrought objects retain in their being and shape the human purpose for which they were made, and thus retain a kind of human-ness. The rug on the floor, as a humanly-wrought fundament, retains the impress of the hands that have woven it and the footsteps of those who have walked on it, even when I am the only person left in the room.

The object and subject appear to be distinct things. But they are bound to one another in that the cultural object delivers to me, the perceiving subject, another subject, though he is general, diffuse, indistinct. The object thus starts to resemble a subject in two ways. First, the shape of the object recalls the shape of the human who made it for the human who will use it. Second, the object does not just retain the ghostly trace of this human-ness but projects it out toward the world. Each manmade object, Merleau-Ponty says, "spreads round it an atmosphere of humanity." The difference between object and subject is hard to place, since the object keeps recalling subjects, anonymous others. In fact, it is not clear if the anonymity belongs to the objects themselves or is in fact only borrowed from the human realm. Sometimes it seems as if the anonymity belongs to the ambiguously present subjects who may once have inhabited or will someday also move through the space in which the object now rests. The object is then the carrier but not the source of the anonymity. Such an object would have anonymous life in the same way that the roots of a plant have the soil. When pulled from the ground, the roots of a plant are surrounded by a ball of earth, because the roots are grabbing hold and giving form to an otherwise formless something not the same as they themselves. Sometimes anonymity is the name Merleau-Ponty gives to the means and mode through which perceptions give us the world, as in: "Every perception takes place in an atmosphere of generality and is presented to us anonymously."[20] At other times, anonymity seems to be a property of the object, indissociable from its function, a function that presents us with other human beings.

But only nearly, only almost. The object is cloaking those other beings that it conjures up with anonymity even as it offers them to my perception. When I perceive objects—a bell, a spoon, a pipe—I perceive the other, but only in a general sense. Merleau-Ponty writes: "In the cultural object I feel the close presence of others beneath a veil of anonymity."[21] Perception, for Merleau-Ponty, is not the same as thinking: "In perception we do not think the object and we do not think ourselves thinking it, we are given over to the object and we merge into this body which is better informed than we are about the world, and about the motives we have and the means at our disposal for synthesizing it."[22] The object I perceive becomes a body into which I merge.

o o o

We will see in the next chapter how cultural objects can not only come to stand in for gender or sexuality but actually become them. The ambiguous relation between the cultural object and the human subject becomes still more ambiguous with Merleau-Ponty's suggestion that the object can also be . . . another subject. And not simply another object, but the cultural object par excellence. "The very first of all cultural objects, and the one by which all the rest exist, is the body of the other person as the vehicle of a form of behavior."[23] We are suddenly in a world that has been denuded of all of its objects save one: the body of the other. That other body exists for me in order to transmit its behavior to me through my perception.

Anonymity is being worked through in such fine grain in this section of the *Phenomenology* in order that Merleau-Ponty might consider what is sometimes referred to in philosophy, with a rather terrifying opacity, "the problem of others." That merely the *ontological being* of others—not others behaving badly or others who are evil or others who cause me trouble, but just the bare fact of others—says something about the discipline no doubt, and certainly the extent to which thinking about intersubjectivity and intercorporeality is a comparatively staggering challenge. Merleau-Ponty's intervention in this debate, and arguably the most significant intervention of the *Phenomenology of Perception* as a whole, is to replace the conception of consciousness as constituting its world with a philosophy of consciousness as that which perceives its world.[24] Merleau-Ponty reorganizes Descartes in insisting that it is not that I project the world, it is that I take it in. And what this reordering, this move from a constituting to a perceptual consciousness, does is give me the other as well as giving me the world. In order to explain the radical shift that this entails, Merleau-Ponty uses the example of a baby: if I playfully pretend to bite a baby's finger, it will open its mouth and attempt to bite, too.[25] In this case, anonymity describes the hinge between Merleau-Ponty and the baby, the fact that they both share the lifeworld, and the anonymity of being allows for a kind of transitivity whereby the baby understands the congruence of its face and his, even before it has a distinctly felt sense of its own.

Two questions might be asked here. First, what *does* this have to do with gender, for our purposes, since Merleau-Ponty does not bring the two together? Echoes of this moment between adult and infant abound in contemporary thinking about infantile relations and gender. Take, for example, Jessica Benjamin in *The Bonds of Love*, in which infant and mother undergo mutual mirroring, which is about recognition, care, and gender. The *Phenomenology of Perception* offers a different scene, with male Merleau-Ponty and the resolutely nongendered baby, where what the baby is feeling inside its own body is the feeling of itself as another, or another as itself. "Biting has immediately, for it an intersubjective significance. It perceives its intentions in its body and my body with its own, and thereby my intentions in its own body."[26] An obvious feminist rejoinder might be: yes, mutuality is well and good, but the fact that Merleau-Ponty is writing gender out of this scene does not mean it is not there. A second, and perhaps still more significant question: anonymity thus described sounds like a happy condition in which I and the other and the world all exist in a mutually beneficial enmeshment. How can anonymity help us think about what happens when that enmeshment is not so happy, when I am locked into the tissue of the world with another who abrades me, injures me, or worse?

V. ANONYMITY AND GENDER

Merleau-Ponty's comments on anonymity have been put to various uses by philosophers thinking about gender. Drawing on them to posit a form of sexuality that exists prior to gender differentiation, Sylvia Stoller argues that the experience of anonymous sexuality and anonymous temporality demonstrate that sexual difference is "an ongoing process of differentiation."[27] Sara Heinamaa uses Merleau-Ponty's theory of anonymity and the matter of drives to argue the opposite,that the central feature of anonymity is that it is *not* differentiated, or at least not by gender. She is interested to show that Merleau-Ponty's conception of anonymity, drawn from Husserl, is not used in opposition to or as a lever against personal subjectivity, as we have already seen. For Merleau-Ponty anonymity is rather "an extension of Husserl's genetic theory of sedimentation," a broadening of the purview of those things that, though repetition and habituation, become us.[28] For Husserl, the sedimentation of actions into subjects is the accretion and transformation of judgments and acts—products of the will—into persons. Merleau-Ponty's extension is his insistence that anonymity becomes sedimented as not merely this layer of willed acts but, more fundamentally, the stratum that underlies those acts. As Heinamaa puts it:

> Merleau-Ponty calls "personal" the layer of subjectivity that is based on decisions, volitions, and judgments, and "anonymous" the layer that is formed in perceptions, motions, and feelings. My main argument is that both levels are *included* in the *Gestaltung* that Husserl calls the "transcendental person." Accordingly, both levels—the level of explicitly egological decisions and volitional acts, and the level of anonymous operations—contribute to the establishment of sexual difference.[29]

Heinamaa thus recruits Husserl and Merleau-Ponty in order to offer a theory of sexual difference in which the volitional and the nonvolitional are intertwined. To

Merleau-Ponty's distinction between the anonymous and the personal, she attaches Husserl's theory of genetic phenomenology, the temporal establishment of meaning through the sedimentation or repeated acts of will and judgment. This genetic phenomenology, she suggests, offers a way of thinking about sexual difference as a *style* rather than an empirical fact of biology, hormones, or the like. "My crucial idea," she ways, "is that Husserl's personalistic concepts of style and type offer the possibility of formulating the question of sexual identity and sexual difference in a radically philosophical way."[30]

Heinamaa's radical philosophizing of sexual difference, then, appeals to Merleau-Ponty's concept of anonymity and also to Husserl's genetic phenomenology. This introduces something of a puzzle, however, one that attends attempts to think the transcendental and the contingent together. Husserl's conception of style relies on the sedimented acts of an individual, acts that accrue to form an individual person, but that might have been arranged or performed differently, resulting in an entirely different style and thus an entirely different person. The location of all of this labor is decidedly at the *personal* level. It is what makes me different from anyone else, even in close temporal and physical proximity, or indeed different from who I would have been had I been born at another moment in time. Merleau-Ponty's anonymity, however, exists in another realm entirely. It is *prepersonal*; it is not dependent on the me-ness of me, even if the use I make of that anonymous bodily experience accrues to and forms that me-ness. Merleau-Ponty also has a philosophy of bodily style, and a precisely formulated one, which he articulates most explicitly in his aesthetic writings, as discussed in chapter 2.[31] But as we have also seen, in his treatment of anonymity in *Phenomenology of Perception*, he emphasizes those aspects of being that are prepersonal, that lie below the level of the individuated subject, below selfhood. Anonymity describes the being that I share with the rest of the world, upon which any further articulated notion of individuation from it must rest. How then ought we understand the interplay of style and anonymity? Where and how do these different spheres of action intersect, if they do? If we return to the realm of everyday usage, style and anonymity would seem to be united only in their opposition to one another, though that opposition might also be a uniting force that binds them inseparably to one another. The realm of aesthetics can offer examples here, as, for instance, in the way that the style of a piece of artwork tends to be most intensely scrutinized when the author of a work or works is anonymous or suspect.

Heinamaa offers us resources for thinking the join between anonymity, phenomenology, and gender. What might be said of the *style* of Latisha's gender? And does understanding gender as a style offer any benefit that might offset the obvious risk that it runs of collapsing gender into mere theatricality or willed performance? The case testimony provides many different assessments of Latisha's gender, offered by scores of classmates, teachers, neighbors, strangers. It became clear throughout the trial that Latisha was taunted and teased for the way she lived her gender, for its style. The disciplining aspirations of her schoolmate's taunting and her teacher's warnings sometimes seemed to have the effect of provoking Latisha to proudly assert her gender. And it sometimes succeeded by triturating her gender back in line with normative expectations, as it did on the last day of her life. As we saw in the last chapter, on February 12, 2008, Latisha came to school looking like a boy. In the words of the Maeve Fox, "He has no makeup, no hair, no boots, no earrings, nothing." With this statement Fox does not mean that Larry has no hair, though that is how it is described when it is unmodified toward the feminine. The district attorney says, "He is wearing nothing," which does not mean that "he" came to school naked, but that "he" was wearing the unremarkable attire and accessories of masculinity, where masculinity is the unmarked term that "passes" as invisible. Wearing nothing no makeup no hair no identifying features. Perfectly anonymous.

VI. AN ENDING

Let us conclude by returning to Susan Crowley's testimony.

> BRAMSON: After [Larry's remark about crochet] you counseled him.
>
> CROWLEY: Yes. And anytime something like that would come up I would hold him back afterwards and say, Larry, you are doing it again. I think Larry wanted to not do it he was just looking for attention and guidance all the time. He could not distinguish between good and bad attention.
>
> BRAMSON: Were those frequent?
>
> CROWLEY: They were. He would say things off topic that other kids would not talk about.

Bramson then asks Mrs. Crowley if Latisha was "cross dressing" at this time. Crowley answers:

> CROWLEY: He didn't cross dress but did accessorize. I would have to say: Larry. He would have a scarf tied

at a jaunty angle and I would have to say: Larry. A
feminine looking scarf and I would say; take that off
sweetheart that is not part of the uniform. And he
would without comment. And I would ask him later
where did you get that and he would say a girlfriend.
And chunky jewelry and I would say take it off but he
would comply.

BRAMSON: The scarves, was that part of the dress code
or just your class?

CROWLEY: It was always being tweaked a little bit and
nothing was ever being enforced. . . . But I didn't
know any other kids that wore scarves. Ever. But I
didn't know if it was prohibited or not.

BRAMSON: Why?

CROWLEY: He was drawing negative attention to himself. And I wanted him to be happy and successful
and I wanted him to be himself but junior high is not
the place for that. I tell the girls that too, button two
more of those buttons.

BRAMSON: Did he comply?

CROWLEY: Yes always: ok Mrs. Crowley. He did not
wear it again in front of me. I think he did value my
opinion and wanted to please me and he knew that
I had good common sense and had his interests at
heart. Kids at that age try out all sorts of stuff and they
need someone to tell them what is appropriate and
not appropriate.

BRAMSON: At the end of seventh grade, did you continue to have concerns for him regarding his attention
seeking behavior?

CROWLEY: Yes. He had not made very much progress
regarding being able to monitor those behavior issues.
It was a self-destructive kind of behavior. He was a

lonely kid and he complained on a daily basis that
other kids teased and harassed them.

To return to Maurice Natanson: things have gone wrong.
In Mrs. Crowley's telling of events, Larry could see her
heart, understood that she was looking after him, and
complied with her requests because he admired her common sense. Common sense has stirred. Mrs. Crowley had
good common sense and was trying to impart that good
sense to Larry; it was her good common sense that caused
her to tell Larry to remove his jewelry, untie his scarf.
And it was her good common sense, if not Larry's, to Mrs.
Crowley's mind, that led him to comply.

What common sense seems not to address, seems not
to be able to see at all, are the actions of those children—
good, compliant, appropriate children—who were teasing
and harassing Latisha. The common nature of common
sense, paradoxically, insures that the actions of those
who participate in that shared consensus are able to escape scrutiny. Latisha could not distinguish between good
and bad attention, Mrs. Crowley asserted repeatedly, although Latisha had just told her about the bad attention
from other students, unwanted and unrelenting. And she
described Latisha as wanting to please her, as comply-
ing rather than acting out in order that she be looked on
favorably, thus demonstrating an ability to discern good
from bad attention and wanting Mrs. Crowley's good attention. She says: "I would have to say: Larry." And she
says this name, says it again, says it over and over, recalling
Latisha to proper gender with the proper masculinity of
this name. She appends the masculine proper name to the
scarf, the crochet, the jewelry, hailing him repeatedly—
Larry—spurred by her discomfort and unease. The scarf

is not specified as a woman's scarf but is still marked as transgressively gendered, with Crowley pointing not to its materiality but to *the way it was tied* that marks it as such.

There is a dual movement to anonymity and loss in this case. In everyday terms, if we are speaking about the loss of anonymity, we are characterizing the conspicuousness of Latisha's gender presentation. That conspicuousness was the target of Mrs. Crowley's observations and interventions. It was also mentioned in a casual way by other participants in the trial, who remarked that "everyone knew who Larry was," or that when Latisha walked down the hall, even before she could be seen, "you could hear him coming." Latisha stood out from the other students. She did not blend in. She did not have the cover of anonymity as she moved through her day, moved through the school. She was not enmeshed in the seamless, unthought, uninterrogated context of the world. Yet if we draw on Natanson's language, the loss of anonymity also describes something about the teachers. It describes what happened to them once they were themselves no longer enmeshed in seamless everydayness, once they were broken out of it by some event, some object, some person. "It is characteristic of the natural attitude," Schütz says, "that it takes the world and its objects for granted until counterproof imposes itself."[32] Latisha became, in effect, a gendered counterproof, disrupting the teachers' shared thesis about the nature of gendered personhood. Latisha appeared as an affront to their certainties about gender and about the world, an affront that they were unable to incorporate into their understanding. In order to resist that affront, even as they were seeing her, they refused to see her.

This matter of attention is where anonymity in its colloquial sense and anonymity in its Merleau-Pontian sense converge. Latisha is understood to be drawing attention to herself, a formulation that transforms the behavior of others into Latisha's willed action. The targeting of Latisha, by the teachers with discipline and by the classmates with taunting and violence, is justified on the basis of her lack of anonymity, and also *results in* the loss of that anonymity. Brandon asserts that "everyone knew" who Latisha was. And that no one liked her. Latisha's lack of anonymity rendered a retreat into pre-personal anonymity impossible. There was no moment during the school day in which she could sink into the simplicity of bodily rhythm and existence. There was no retreat inward toward solaces of undifferentiated being-with-others that characterizes anonymous life. The role of common sense is to insist that this loss of anonymity was function of Latisha's own behavior. To assert, once again, that she was, once again, asking for it.

OBJECTS

I. THE DRESS AND THE BOOTS

On July 26, 2011, Defense Attorney Robyn Bramson asked Judge Charles Campbell to direct Maeve Fox to produce several pieces of physical evidence for the defense team's use during testimony. The district attorney agreed, and a number of large paper bags made their way into the courtroom, each containing something that had belonged to Latisha King. One of those bags held a pair of brown, heeled boots. Another held a backpack containing several items, including makeup and lipstick. And another contained a strapless, green homecoming dress. The defense team requested these items, procured them, and cut them out of the brown paper evidence bags into which they had been carefully sealed. Showed them to the witness. Walked them back and forth in front of the members of the jury. In requesting that these objects be brought into the courtroom, the defense team demonstrated its belief that the physical presence of these objects was able to convey something that a photographic representation or verbal description of them could not. In putting these things in front of the jury, the lawyers were asking these objects to disclose their meaning, a disclosure, and perhaps even a meaning, that became possible only in the physical presence of the object.

As we have seen, throughout this trial gender was read from the expression, rather than the materiality, of the body. Latisha King's gender was read from her gestures, her comportment, her movement. But at several crucial moments during the trial, gender was also discerned *from* and determined *by* objects. At first glance, these would seem to be opposed, even mutually canceling, understandings of what gender is. If gender inheres in gestures, than it is ephemeral, temporally undecidable, immaterial, whereas objects are substantial, concrete, solid, material. Gender as gesture is alive; gender as an object, one would presume, less so. But the congruence between understanding gender as an object and gender as a gesture is that in this case both views of gender were presented as if they had a meaning that language had no part in mediating. That is, both gesture and object were understood to speak for themselves. What meaning did the dress have for the defense lawyers? For those assembled in the courtroom? And for the jury? That meaning gathered momentum and strengthened with the object's repeated invocation, as the green dress and the high-heeled boots were mentioned hundreds of times during the trial. One would perhaps have to look to a rape trial to find such analogously scrupulous and obsessive legal attention to what the victim had been wearing before the assault, the meticulous attempt to discern just how "provocative" that dress might have been.

In court, the green dress is lifted carefully out of the bag, in a gesture that looked to my eyes more like fear than reverence: less how you'd handle a precious, breakable thing, more how you would lift a wild animal that was unconscious but not all the way dead. As if that object, which was once almost-animate once animated on Latisha's body, had a power that was not quite extinguished by the death of the one who once wore it, the one who wore it once. And the power that it had was the ability to confer gender, to enact gender, to become gender itself. Latisha's gender was not a matter of her sexed body, but rather the conjoined effect of her bodily movement and the material signifiers of femininity that were worn on, though not part of, her body. The earrings. The makeup. The scarf. The dress and the boots. The defense attorneys invoke them over and over: the dress and the boots, the dress and the boots. As witnesses were asked again and again: *Larry King, did you see him wear a dress? Where? When? How many times? What did it look like? What color was it? The boots? What color were they? Were they past the ankle? Up to the knee? How high up the leg did they go? How high were the heels? Two inches? Three? Four?* At least one of the students in testimony, when asked about Larry's dress, corrects the defense attorney: *I was talking about the way he dressed, not a dress. I never seen no dress.* The student makes it clear that when he is talking about Latisha he is describing an overall fact of her being, a style, rather than a particular object, a dress. But the defense demands that the dress be documented and detailed and recalled and then produced, so it could tell its particular kind of truth.

If the dress was an object that was understood to be saying something about gender and also about sexuality, a something said through simply its physical presence, its objecthood, the question becomes: What was it that the dress said? What message did it offer so wordlessly yet so eloquently that at least one person in the courtroom gasped as the dress was brought out of the paper evidence bag? The gasp would seem to be a response to something surprising, shocking, or out of place in the presence of the dress. The dress in the hands of the defense attorneys speaks its meaning forth in this way, as an object that names Latisha as a culpable subject, announcing her perversion.

But the dress was held in other hands as well. And spoke other meanings when traveling through those other hands. What meaning did it have for Latisha? One child gave testimony about the moment when their teacher, Dawn Boldrin, made a gift of the dress to Latisha.

Q. BY DEFENSE ATTORNEY SCOTT WIPPERT: Did she give it to Larry in front of everyone or did Larry get it from her and then tell others about it?

ANDREA: No. She had given it to him like in a bag. I think it was before class like.

Q: In a bag, is that what you said?

A: I think.

Q: Do you know what kind of bag it was?

A. It was like a plastic bag. I think she had it in there. She didn't give it to him openly. It was like in a bag like, "Oh, here you go."

Q: Okay. But you learned that from Larry?

A: Yeah, I saw it, so I was like, "Oh, okay."

Q: Okay. So if she gave it to him in a bag, how did you see it? Did Larry pull it out and show people?

A: Like I said, he pulled it out, but he wasn't like telling everyone like, "Oh, look." He was just like looking at it like smiling and talking to Miss Boldrin. And people would comment like, "Oh, that's a nice dress," like—it was just like that.[1]

The witness describes the moment that the green dress is handed over to Latisha. It is a gift from her teacher, and from her teacher's daughter, who had worn the dress to homecoming and would not wear it again because, as Boldrin put it, "Everybody knows you don't re-use your dress." Latisha is gifted the dress through this hand-me-down ritual, which includes it within, rather than setting it outside of, the lines of transmission through which femininity is generationally taught and conferred, gifted and imposed. And the dress is an object that is soaked with meaning, tiny in size and heavy with significance, in the school and also in the courtroom. As Merleau-Ponty writes, discussing objects and their transmission of meaning: "The significance of a thing inhabits that thing as the soul inhabits the body: it is not behind appearances. . . . Prior to and independently of other people, the thing achieves that miracle of expression: an inner reality which reveals itself externally, a significance which descends into the world and begins its existence there, and which can be fully understood only when the eyes seek it in its own location."[2] In this case, the location of the thing was inside another thing. The dress was inside a bag, not the brown paper evidence bag of the courtroom but a brightly colored bag in which Dawn had placed her daughter's dress so that she might bring it to school for Latisha. It was a pink bag with leopard print and a boa-like trim on the top. The object it contained sat inside it, with more than one meaning, more than two, full of them, replete with them. Even the bag that held the dress, functioning as a vehicle to carry the recently discarded and soon-to-be-beloved object from Dawn Boldrin's house to her classroom, refused to speak singular meaning. It was, at once, whispering its discretion and shouting its fabulousness.

II. TRUE SIZE

> BRAMSON: I am holding up in front of you a green
>   dress. Do you recall this?
> BOLDRIN: I do.

In the witness box, Boldrin starts to weep.

> BOLDRIN: I do, yes. It was my daughter's tenth grade
>   homecoming dress.
> BRAMSON: Are you okay?
> BOLDRIN: Yeah, I'm okay. I'm sorry.
> [Pause.]
> BOLDRIN: Yeah. You know. Girls.[3]

As she tries to recover herself, dabbing at her eyes with
Kleenex, Boldrin apologizes for losing her composure, an
apology and an explanation contained in the single word.
Girls. Girls will be girls. Girls (female gendered beings)
will be girls (overcome with emotion). Weepy. Stricken.
She names herself as a girl, apologizing to the defense attorney who is a girl, in describing her efforts as she and her
own girl helped Latisha become a girl. Boldrin continues:

> BOLDRIN: My daughter gave that dress to Larry. I gave it
>   to him, she gave him the dress.
> BRAMSON: It was from her and you were the one who
>   delivered it?
> BOLDRIN: Yes.
> BRAMSON: It was a long time ago, but do you remember
>   when?
> BOLDRIN: I don't know. I'm an English teacher not a
>   math teacher. . . . It was the Friday before.[4]

As Boldrin speaks, crying is heard in the gallery. Another
"girl." It is Kendra, Brandon's mother, weeping.

> BOLDRIN: This is the picture of Larry holding the dress.
>   I took it with my cell phone and sent it to my daugh-

ter because he wanted to thank her for giving him the dress.[5]

Boldrin is a girl transmitting thanks from one girl to another. The picture is projected onto the screen set up in the courtroom. Latisha, smiling, holding up a green homecoming dress. An expression of joy and gratitude. Boldrin explains that she sent the photograph so that her daughter could see Latisha's happiness at receiving the gift. Robyn Bramson begins to cry.

BRAMSON: Did you say that you . . . so you took the photograph on your cell phone?

BOLDRIN: Yes.

BRAMSON: And then did you send it to your daughter?

BOLDRIN: I sent it to my daughter because my daughters—I don't know. I think as a mother I tried to raise my daughters to be good people, and I had noted to them why Larry was in foster care because he was being beat for being—[6]

Boldrin is cut off by an objection from the prosecution, an objection that is itself interrupted by a sound in the gallery. Gregory King, Latisha's adoptive father, stands up, slams down his seat, and stomps out of the courtroom. Once again, the transgression is unspeakable, unable to be heard, will not be countenanced by Gregory King. His departure from the courtroom, abrupt, violent, is an attempt to stop or squelch the invocation of queerness that was about to issue from the witness box, even as his act mimetically reproduces the accusation it was meant to silence. *Larry was in foster care because he was being beat for being . . .*

The judge sustains the objection, and chastises Boldrin for being nonresponsive.

JUDGE CAMPBELL: Ms. Boldrin, you need to just answer the questions.

Gregory King walks back into the courtroom and barks to the rest of the King family, his wife, her mother, and their other child: "We are leaving the courtroom. Let's go." All the Kings file out. As they exit, Latisha's grandmother says something to a girl in the very back row of the gallery, a hissed or muttered something that I cannot hear from where I am seated. The girl starts crying. After the Kings depart, the courtroom is quiet, except for the girl in the back row, sobbing. She is Dawn Boldrin's daughter. She is led out of the courtroom.

Dawn Boldrin noted that the green dress was very small because her daughter was very small. "She's a double zero so that lets you know how little he was," Boldrin said, referring to Latisha.[7] The matter of Latisha's physical size was brought up frequently by the prosecution. The defense did not much remark on Latisha's physical size, but emphasized repeatedly that she "took up a lot of room." At 5'4" and 111 pounds, Latisha was small. Certainly much smaller than Brandon McInerney. But her presence was characterized throughout the testimony as big. She was described as taking up a lot of space. And this taking up of space was not a fact of her physical size, but an effect of magnification enacted by her gestural life. Some of this largeness was undoubtedly projection; the gendered style of her embodiment made her "stick out" and marked her as an object of fascination and contempt and pity and fear and hatred. Those who hated or feared her justified that hatred and fear by constituting her as big, as threatening.[8] In characterizing Latisha's presence as big and her gender presentation as threatening, those who were aggressive toward her were constituting their own aggression as defensive, as we have already seen. But part of that becoming larger, of exceeding her physical size, came from Latisha herself. Many teachers and students described Latisha's behavior as changing in the ten days before her death. This behavior included wearing girls' shoes and eye shadow, and possibly hair gel, but also exceeded the physical objects that metonymically came to *be* her gender. The witnesses at the trial did not give a unified account of this change, either its source or nature, but Latisha was described as transforming into a person who was newly confident, proud, unashamed, bold, standing up to those who were teasing and bullying her.

What does it mean to *take up a lot of room*? And how do we make determinations of size?[9] Merleau-Ponty has much to say on the matter of size, on the impossibility and necessity of determining what one's size is, where size is an experiential rather than a physical fact. We might see Freud as continually addressing the same question in the psychic realm—what is my true size? For the psychoanalyst and the phenomenologist both, the question of one's true size is always a matter of one's relation to other things and other people. And when we cannot figure out the answer to this question—what is my true size?—we suffer. And sometimes we cause others to suffer. Merleau-Ponty suggests that the size of a person or an object is never singularly true, giving as one example "the road close up is not more true than the road far away." Because of his fascination with the impossibility of this determination, Merleau-Ponty was compelled by those instances in which it is difficult or impossible to determine what a thing's true size is. He suggests that children, too, are compelled by such difficult-to-determine objects. In his essay "Indirect Language and the Voices of Silence," he uses the example of the moon as such an object. It is something that exists for the child, is perceived by the child, yet exists outside of her, at the outer limits of her world, beyond the reach of her grasp. She can neither move closer nor farther away from it; she cannot change its relative size, its appearance, by changing her own relation to it, in the way that she would with a house or a stone or a cat. The moon is a thing presenting a certain fixity that, paradoxically, gives it the appearance of movement. As I walk down a country road at night, the moon that illuminates the gravel in front of me seems to follow me, accompanying my movement with its own and stopping when I pause.

III. ULTRA-THINGS

Merleau-Ponty calls the moon and other objects of this kind an "ultra-chose," an ultra-thing. The word describes things that are present to a child but ambiguously so, within her perception but out of her grasp. He draws the concept from Henri Wallon in order to challenge Jean Piaget and counter a representationalist model of the childhood mind. Ultra-things are things that appear, but outside of the orbit and beyond the reach of rationalist and familiar explanations of the world with which the child is familiar. He writes: "Borrowing from a profound notion introduced by Wallon, the presence in the child's experience of 'ultra-things' which are certain beings that exist for children but are not within their scope or reach. Such beings are not fully grasped by simply looking at them, and children cannot change them by willing or by moving their bodies. In short, they are things that they are not able to fully observe. The significance of this notion has not been fully recognized."[10] The child is not able to fully observe an ultra-thing, he cannot test or manipulate it. It remains in some essential way out of his grasp and out of his comprehension. The earth and the sky are exemplary "ultra-things'" for the child. An ultra-thing is something in which a rational account cannot quite compel my belief. Children can believe in such things "only with their lips," Merleau-Ponty says. The object itself might be familiar, like the moon, but the explanation for its existence or behavior will not be.

So an ultra-thing can be an object like the moon, and more expansively a being, like the child that my parent once was. As he expands the roster of things that might be classified as ultra-things, Merleau-Ponty also enlarges the circle of those who might *perceive* ultra-things, suggesting that adults, too, have them. And like the sky for the child, or the child that her parent once was, the ultra-thing for an adult is outside of his grasp, essentially opaque to him, elides his rational thought, and is only believed in "with [the] lips." But the ultra-things that adults have are neither objects nor beings but *states*. The paradigmatic examples, Merleau-Ponty says, are one's birth and one's death. The ultra-thing is that which forms the very outside edges of the horizon of his experience.

In the King case, we might consider that the norms of gender function as an ultra-chose. It is a thing about which the child does not have a thesis, an explanation. It is a thing that is inescapably present, that forms the horizon of his experience, yet is not manipulable, not capable of being moved under his control. It is present everywhere, seemingly inescapable, yet the rules that govern its appearance, division, and enforcement are obscure. Latisha King clearly had an experience of her own gender, a felt sense that compelled a performance of gender that was at odds with the dictates of her family and her school. And her performance of gender breached the rules that her teachers and classmates seemed so eager to enforce. Was Latisha, then, childlike in her relation to gender? Was she operating without a thesis about it, while those around her understand gender in a more adult way? I would suggest that, in fact, the opposite may be true. Gender for Latisha may have been a realm characterized by a kind of magical thinking to which Merleau-Ponty refers when he describes the ultra-thing. That magical thinking would believe the heeled boots to have the power to confer gender, to gift their wearer with girlhood. Or inexpertly applied eye shadow. Or a green homecoming dress. But the response of the adults around her showed that she was not wrong in this thinking. Indeed the drive to *regulate* Latisha, to prevent her performance of her feminine gender, and to insist that Larry was a boy not a girl, thus must not be allowed to put shadow on his eyelids gel in his hair heels on his feet, demonstrates that the adults were engaging in thinking that was still more magical than the gender-variant child they were trying to straighten out, and that they clung to this thinking without the guidance of an internal conviction of a felt sense of gender spurring them on. That is: the adults seemed simultaneously convinced that Larry was a boy and thus could not wear girl's boots and that those gendered objects were totems invested with such power to transform their wearer and also to contaminate those nearby that those objects needed to be forbidden. "Larry," said one teacher, "needed to be stopped."

Gender may be more of an ultra-thing for the adults who sought to police it than it was for Latisha, who lived in and through it. That the teachers who policed her gender also have a gender was invisible to them. The contention in this case was that when Larry walked down the hallway in his boots, he was making an issue of his gender. As Samantha, Brandon McInerney's girlfriend, said, Larry put on a dress and in doing so "Larry was shoving it in everyone's face." The dress became the gender; the gender became an object; the object became a weapon. Latisha may have thought magically about her own gender, but the myths of gender under which the adults in her life operated are much more pernicious and *less* attuned to the realities of gender than Latisha's fantasies. Those myths: that gender is binary, and that any deviation from that binary is wrong, and bad, and dangerous. And that it was Latisha who represented the danger and not those who sought to stop her, fully and finally.

IV. PHENOMENOLOGICAL ETHICS

What can we say about the response to Latisha's gender presentation within the school and its representation in the courtroom? And what can we say about what it *should* have been? Phenomenology is generally understood to belong to the province of the descriptive rather than the normative, the *is* rather than the *should*. The question then becomes, how can phenomenology grasp hold of the ethical? What might it have to offer the philosophical enterprise of thinking through ethics, if it is not able to supply norms? This question of phenomenology's proper objects, or ethics' proper methods, is raised by much recent work in phenomenology, as we can see in recent work on Husserl's ethics,[11] in Lester Embree's volume on the phenomenology of moral philosophy, and in Kevin Hermberg and Paul Gyllenhammer's still more recent collection *Phenomenology and Virtue Ethics*, in which John Drummond crisply describes the matter thusly: "One could argue that phenomenology cannot bridge the gap between the descriptive and the normative, and can therefore tell us nothing about ethics."[12] He does not agree of course; rather, he describes the problem in a nutshell. If the phenomenological method is description, it is not a sufficiently wide arena in which to consider questions of the ethical if the method were *merely* description. The question then becomes, what might those descriptive practices offer if we want to use phenomenology in order to gain traction on ethical issues? If we have ethical questions that we want to pose to phenomenology, what can phenomenology do with description to help us engage the ethical?

One way to think this is to consider the ways in which the merely descriptive always carries a normative valence, even if that normative charge is obscured. We can see this at work in the visual realm, which one could convincingly argue has historically been phenomenology's favored mode of investigation. The specular may be the most common method—and arguably the most familiar object—of phenomenology. The realm of the specular, though, is never purely, or even mostly, about appearance understood as either a passive taking-in or a neutral, perspectival-less unfolding. Because seeing is always embodied, power, relation, violence, ethics, and intersubjectivity are there, from the start. And surely even before that.

One of the things phenomenology teaches us is that observation, that description, is just as likely to get us to a place of unknowing as to a place of knowing. Phenomenology as method can lead us to a place of greater knowing, but it can also have as one of its effects a loosening or an undoing of what we know. To withhold one's judgment, to refuse to rush to a conclusion, to resist one's habits of certainty—these all seem to be strategies keyed to the limits of knowing, which are always at stake in unknowing, yet there is something more, something additional, at work in it. Unknowing is not merely a marking of the limits of knowledge, but a mode or an activity that involves or engages something beyond that marking of limits. Unknowing is not only a negative withholding, but also an active—if not quite affirmative—*something*, and it is temporally stranger than uncertainty. To be uncertain is to vacillate on the threshold of certainty, while to unknow is to revise or undo knowledge that I already have, perhaps to question the epistemological regime that brought that knowing about in the first place.

Another answer to the question of the relation between the phenomenological and the ethical is gestured to by Werner Marx, whose book *Towards a Phenomenological Ethics* asks if there might be an approach to ethics that is nonmetaphysical. He dispatches with the descriptive versus normative impasse by suggesting that the object to be defined can be an *ethos*: "One can forgo the name ethics and be content to speak of 'descriptions of ethos.' . . . We find the appropriate method of describing an ethos within the realm of non-metaphysical thought in a phenomenological explication."[13] As Marx explains, when we describe, we are not marking down facts or events but finding, also, something else. "For phenomenology may not simply 'depict' what is experienced in each respective case. It rather attempts to interpret a structural whole in such a way that it does not grasp an individual entity, but the *being* of this entity."[14] This distinction needs some parsing, since it is not clear what inquiry after the being of the entity would look like, apart from and other than ontological inquiry, or how we would have escaped the realm of metaphysics with this kind of inquiry. Marx suggests that the end goal of a phenomenological ethics is the cultivation of compassion—of compassion for others, a fellow-feeling with our fellow beings. But there is, too, a hint of reflexivity about the suggestion, that compassion also turns inward, that contemplation of my own mortality might also lead me to be more compassionate toward myself.

What, then, is a description of ethos? The example Marx gives is the human experience of mortality, which we experience as one side of our Being. In this view, I am always reaching toward mortality but never touching it; it is the inner lining of my experience of life, where the separation between the two divides me into distinct regions of being. We are able to experience that mortality through our *human comportment*, emphasizing the centrality of the body in all of our relations. Comportment is what joins me to the world, and it is equally what joins me with other, whom I then experience as the other side of my Being, as *sociality*. These twin poles of human existence, mortality and sociality, are, Marx claims, joined in the human person by comportment, which offers access to and is the medium of both. And sociality becomes something that is indistinguishable from life itself.

V. IF SOMETHING WASN'T DONE SOON
After the trial was over, several jurors spoke on camera about the reasons they were unwilling to find Brandon

guilty of first-degree murder and had wished instead to find him guilty of second-degree murder or of voluntary manslaughter. Rosalie Black, an alternate juror, stated, "I don't think it was first degree murder. It *was* premeditated."[15] With that single statement Black pithily demonstrated that she did not comprehend the most fundamental matter the jury was charged to consider, since a determination of the latter, premeditation, in this case necessitated the former, a finding of first-degree murder. The instructions to the jury did not ask them to adjudicate guilt or innocence; innocence is not a plausible plea when the victim is unarmed, unaware, and shot in the back of the head, twice, in front of a room full of witnesses. Rather, the jury was to determine what kind of guilty verdict would be returned. In the end, the hung jury and the resulting mistrial ensured that no kind of guilty verdict was returned.

In this frank conversation among jurors, extraordinarily captured by director Marta Cunningham in the documentary film *Valentine Road*, three jurors described what it was that led them to decide, or to refrain from deciding, in the way they had. They were at some pains to communicate that it was not homophobia that determined their decision. The problem with Larry, they explained, was not that he was gay. They knew that Brandon had no problem with Larry's sexual orientation because Brandon had no problem with Marina, another student at E.O. Green, who was gay. When the administrators approached Marina and told her she was not allowed to hold hands with her girlfriend at school, she stopped holding hands with her girlfriend. "Marina got it," said one of the jurors, implying that they, too, had no problem with Marina's sexual orientation, and thus, transitively, no problem with anyone else's. Then two of them interject in unison: *"Larry didn't get it."*

What was the nature of this "it" that Latisha didn't get? One might assume that it was the injunction, punishable by violence or even death, against a certain kind of self-expression, that the "good" queer student of color was not punished because she knew when not to express herself, and the "bad" one was because she did not know, or refused to know, or did not let that knowing circumscribe her expression. Yet the jurors were objecting to something still more concrete than this. "It was the high heels, it was the makeup," said one. Thus, it was not the ontological fact of Larry's "gayness" that constituted a problem for either Brandon McInerney or the jurors. It was Latisha's unwillingness to squelch its expression in her gestural life. In that, it was her defiance.[16] But perhaps even more determinatively: *it* was the objects, Latisha's objects. *It* was the high heels, *it* was the makeup.

In the film, the juror names the objects that were paraded solemnly in front of the jury box, the objects with their unmistakable connotation of gender transgression, a naming that confirms the defense decision to show those objects as a canny one. It was those objects that did not just stand in for but actually became gender and also its transgression which are named as the reason, the problem, the thing that turned both Brandon and the jury against Latisha. Because Latisha didn't get it, she was a problem. Because Latisha would not take up less space, she was a problem. Because she was a trans youth of color, she was a problem. As one juror understood it, Latisha's form of dress was actually a form of taunting Brandon. Since the school administrators did not share this view of Latisha's gender expression, would not "help" Brandon with this "harassment," the juror explained, "He was solving a problem." And as Brandon himself put it, in a statement that demonstrates in one turn the social sanction with which he operated leading up to and during the killing and the dispatch with which he sealed Latisha into perfect object-hood before doing so: "I felt like it would make everyone's life at school better. I felt like I was solving a problem and doing the right thing. I didn't even think of killing Larry, just of getting rid of him, and that's how I would get rid of him." The question then emerges: What environment, what context within the school, would lead Brandon Mc-Inerney to the conclusion that he was "doing the right thing" in shooting Latisha King?

The testimony from the teachers at E. O. Green Junior High gives some clue.

VI. RETROACTIVE CROSSING-OUT

In at least two instances, teachers made note of Latisha's appearance in a way that, again, transformed gender expression into aggressive behavior. One teacher, Debi Goldstein, offered the following testimony:

Q: Was there a lot of talk going around the school about Larry King?

A: I did not know the boy's name.

Q: Was there rumbling about a boy who chose to express himself?

A: Yes. Some of the students and teachers were upset about it. . . .

Q: Can you tell us the type of things that you heard about this boy who was choosing to express his potential sexual identity through dress?

Here, as throughout, we see a conflation of sexual identity and gender identity. It passed unremarked, but the prosecutor objected to the last question on the grounds of relevance, and the objection was sustained. The defense tried again:

Q: In your opinion, as the teacher there, did you think that there was anything regarding this boy expressing his sexuality and dressing in the manner that he was that was disrupting to the school?

A: Yes it was.

Q: How?

A: Because the teachers were upset.

Q: Were students upset?

A: The teachers were upset because it was distracting.

Q: Was he a disruption?

A: Yes. He went too far.

Q: And what is it that you saw or noticed that gave you the opinion that he was a disruption?

A: I had an epiphany a week before the shooting. I saw this pretty little girl talking with the students. She had short hair and nice earrings and cute jeans and a beautiful little figure and then she turned around and I saw it was a boy. And I saw that this is Larry, and this was what all the rumblings were about, and now I understand.

Q: Like a fifteen-year-old girl would dress?

A: More like a high school or college student. He dressed to be sexy.

Q: Can you say how he was dressing more like a high school or a college girl?

A: It was the way he put everything together. The way everything was, to his hair to his clothing to his boots

his finger polish. It was more than any of the girls
would do at that age at our school.

Q: So it was more than any other girl at the school?

A: Right.

Q: When you were at E. O. Green did you ever see any
girls dressed like that?

A: Yes. When they would go for graduation they would
dress up really nice and beautiful. But on a regular
school day they don't.

In the scene Debi Goldstein describes, she is approaching
a girl talking to some other students, a girl whose appearance she showers with superlatives: she is a pretty little girl,
her jeans are cute, her earrings are nice, she has a beautiful
little figure. The moment of disorientation and discovery
comes when this girl turns around and, Goldstein says, "I
saw it was a boy." This girl was talking with her classmates,
was not causing trouble; there was no disruption. The disruption occurs only once Goldstein realizes: this is Larry.
She has to reverses her prior assessment of the scene and
see it differently. The tableau that initially struck her as
unremarkable, innocuous, is now revised, and becomes a
problem. She does not single out one element of Latisha's
attire or behavior and name it distressing; rather, she is
distressed by the general gestalt of her gender presentation. As she says, "It is the way that everything was put
together" that was striking about Latisha's appearance.
Note that in this moment it is not the social scene in the
school that is disrupted by Latisha's appearance, though
in other moments it was. What is disrupted is Goldstein's
sense of gender propriety, her understanding of how a girl
should look and how a boy should look, and the "epiphany," in her words, that she experiences the moment

when Latisha turns around, is the dis-orientation of that expectation.

I suggest that we can understand what happened in this moment as something that Husserl has called a *retroactive crossing out.*[17] Suppose, says Husserl, I am looking at a red ball. As I look I have a sense of it, I form an understanding of not just the side of the ball that I see but the thing entire, through mostly unconscious acts of synthesis. But if I turn the ball around, or position myself so that I can look at it from another angle, I can see that the unseen face of the ball that had been turned away from me, is not red and round but in fact green and dented. In that moment, a retroactive crossing out occurs. Rather than functioning in an additive way, rather than merely giving me one more piece of information about the nature of this ball, this new perspective undoes my prior synthesis and strikes out what I thought I knew of the ball. Everything I had known before about the object becomes voided.

We might say that the girl that Debi caught sight of was subject to a retroactive crossing out. Once Debi came to the realization "it's a boy" (Larry), the girl that she saw in front of her (Latisha) was nullified. Indeed we can see instances of this retroactive crossing out all throughout the school, as some of the students and most of the teachers refused Latisha life, withheld recognition from her, sought to void or cancel her existence. Violence against Latisha, daily teasing and name calling, shoving her into the lockers as she passed by, was part of the normative fabric of the school. In this way, Brandon's act was the most extreme example of a process that was going on in a thousand different ways all throughout the school. And Brandon was following, rather than defying, the desires and expectations of his teachers, with their repeated incantation that *Larry had to be stopped.*

One teacher, Shirley Brown, testified in reply to a question about the atmosphere of danger in the school:

Q: Did you, during this period were you in fear for his safety from other boys?
A: I was fearful for his safety, yes. My comment to my principal was that if something wasn't done soon that Larry would be taken behind the back shed of the PE area and beaten to death.

The "something" that needed to be done, however, was not an intervention on Latisha's behalf. Latisha was, in Brown's words "making himself a target," and it was that self-fashioning, which she considered provocative and outrageous, that needed to be stopped. Brown testified that she saw a number of boys chasing Latisha, but that she did nothing. Boys chasing, teasing, harassing, or persecuting Latisha was not the "something" that needed stopping. After the trial was over, Shirley Brown recounted Latisha coming to her and asking for advice. "I knew his inclination. He came to discuss it with me." Inclination: *clino*, to bend. She did not specify which inclination, but her response suggests that Latisha King sought Shirley Brown's counsel because she believed that she was trans, that she felt a gathering momentum of her identity as a girl. As she recounts in *Valentine Road*, this is how she responded:

When Larry asked me what to do about this situation I said: nothing. What to do about this situation is nothing. And to keep it private. And to dwell upon it. Larry shouldn't have expressed himself so blatantly, openly, transsexual. He progressed day by day in his outward appearance as a girl. I do believe in a heaven and a hell, and I do believe Larry honestly did not have a clue, honestly, the consequences of his actions. I relate to Brandon because I could see my own self being in that very same position. I don't know if I would have taken a gun, but a good, swift kick in the butt might work really well.[18]

"Transsexual" here is an adjective describing dress, rather than naming an identity or gender category. "Transsexual" is a term that modifies "expression." Nonetheless, Shirley Brown offers a name that everyone else in the courtroom was invested in withholding. She calls Latisha "transsexual," in an act of naming that she understands to simultaneously mark Latisha as aggressive and also marks her as the proper target of aggression.

Latisha says to Shirley Brown: *I am not Larry, a boy, but Latisha, a girl. What should I do?* And Brown replies: *Nothing. What to do about this situation is nothing.* Brown acknowledges that there is a "situation" with Latisha's gender, but it is a situation for which no action is appropriate, a situation about or in which Latisha should not act. She should do nothing, she should say nothing, and she should "dwell upon it." It is not a *dwelling in* but a motionless *contemplation of* gender that the teacher advises, and the archaic phrasing of her counsel anticipates the biblical feel of the declamation that follows: "I believe in a heaven and a hell," Brown states, intimating the kind of Old Testament wrath that she understands to be waiting if Latisha did not follow her advice, keep quiet, do nothing, stay a boy. *Larry may believe that he is a girl, but I believe in a heaven and a hell.*

If unknowing is one of the goals of a phenomenological ethos, we see here that it cannot be just any unknowing, pointing in any direction. What Shirley Brown is aiming at is to get Latisha to unknow what she believes about herself. A phenomenological ethos of unknowing must instead be reflexive, it must be my goal to unseat my *own* belief through the suspension of what I already think I know. For Shirley Brown, however, it is she who is the knower, and Latisha who does not know, who "honestly did not have a clue." Brown's belief, and her certainty, allow her to nullify Latisha, to subject her to that retroactive crossing out. That crossing out is accompanied by Brown's revisionist fantasy of herself in the very same position as Brandon, as the agent of punishment, enforcing her own certainties about gender with a kick, an assault, a violence that thinks itself merciful, because it is a body and not a gun that is its instrument.

The mirroring between teacher and student, between Shirley Brown and Brandon McInerney, reveals the rather bland and nonspecific language about safety that permeated the trial to have been a screen discourse behind which there lay a much more pointed wish—the wish that Latisha's gender transgressions should be punished with physical assault. Brown's suggestion that the children were not ready for Latisha's gender can thus be seen as a projection of her own discomfort and rage. The school must be safe, made safe from the ostensible danger of Latisha, the unspecified threat that she was understood to represent to unspecified victims. Shirley Brown wanted to beat Latisha up so that the school could be safe, a safety whose purview is thus shown never to have included Latisha herself. And Brandon's discomfort and rage can be seen still more clearly as what it straightforwardly announced itself to be: a response that was not just individual but, importantly, collective, ready to act on the only partially submerged hatred emanating from those who saw Latisha, finally, as the greatest threat to the "safety" of the school.

CODA: TWO DAYS IN FEBRUARY

In this book, I have tried to illuminate the relation between gender identity, sexual identity, and aggression in the courtroom and in the popular imagination through a slow phenomenology of one single case, a case in which the illogics of transphobia, homophobia, and racism were on clear display. Phenomenology, as I have aimed to show, can give us insight into the conditions that enable such an episode of violence, as well as a way of reading its aftermath. It can help us see those things anew, see situations and people that our sedimented habits of thought have prevented us from seeing well, or prevented us from seeing at all. Letting that space of unknowing permeate what we see can offer a more ethical way of relating to otherness.

Latisha King was murdered nearly ten years ago. The public visibility of transpeople, and the recognition of trans identity, have fundamentally shifted our cultural landscape since that time, and we might be tempted to conclude that the case is merely a relic of an earlier, less-enlightened era. Yet many of the presuppositions about gender nonconformity on display in the King case, and the attendant attributions of aggression to the gender nonconforming, are not merely persisting but gathering frightening new momentum in the wake of the Trump presidency, and it remains to be seen what will become of the gains made by the trans community in the coming months and years. The case of Latisha King is not as anachronistic as it should be in our present moment. What does seem true is that the visibility of transpeople has ushered in a new era, one in which their identities are increasingly legible at the same time that there is transphobic backlash against that visibility, powered by what Tobias Wolff has named an "ugly genocidal fantasy" about transpeople.[1] This backlash is weaponizing both visibility and invisibility in order to police, to contest, and to erase the very existence of transpeople.

o o o

On February 22, 2017, as I was completing the writing of this book, the U.S. Department of Education, under the direction of Betsy deVos, and the Justice Department, under the direction of Attorney General Jeff Sessions, co-authored an untitled Dear Colleague letter.[2] The purpose of that letter was to withdraw the policy and guidelines set forth in two previous letters authored by the Obama administration in 2015 and 2016, which directed public schools to treat a "student's gender identity as the student's sex for purposes of Title IX and its implementing regulations." As the May 2016 letter put it, "This means that a school must not treat a transgender student differently from the way it treats other students of the same gender identity." The practical impact of these Obama-era guidelines included mandating, under Title IX, that students be able to use the bathroom and locker room that corresponded to their gender identity, even if it was not the same as their sex assigned at birth. That support was delivered publicly in a press conference held by Attorney General Loretta Lynch on May 9, 2016. In her statements, she specifically addressed the trans community with these words: "We see you, we stand with you, and we will do everything we can to protect you going forward."[3]

The Trump administration's February 22 letter does not anywhere in its two pages mention the word "transgender." It notes that the occasion for its issue was the previous administration's interpretation of Title IX, which "has given rise to significant litigation regarding school restrooms and locker rooms." That earlier interpretation, which the February 22 letter calls "novel," was put forth in guidance documents that, according to the new administration, "did not contain extensive legal analysis," and thus the Department of Education and the Department of Justice rescinded the prior letters "in order to further and more completely consider the legal issues involved." With its withdrawal of protection for transpeople, whom the letter targets yet refuses to name, the Justice Department nullified the support offered by the previous administration.

The legal issues, according to the language of the letter, are the sanctity of sex-segregated facilities, a stated concern shared by a number of recent bills proposed or passed by state legislatures that require transpeople to use the restroom corresponding to the sex designation on their birth certificates. These bills sometimes imply and sometimes state explicitly that they are about the safety of girls and women and are intended to protect them from sexual harassment and assault. (Just as concern about the sanctity of life does not, in the social conservative imagination, extend to the life and well-being of a child once she leaves the womb, concerns that a woman should be protected from sexual harassment or assault seem to vanish once she leaves a sex-segregated restroom.) These include the "Texas Privacy Bill," SB6, which declared itself to be addressing the "privacy" of sex-segregated facilities, and HB2, the North

Carolina "Public Facilities Privacy and Security Act," which was approved into law in 2016. The term "privacy" in these bills has a dual action, naming a right to privacy for women and girls in women's restrooms, a right that the bill aims to protect. But "privacy" is also asserted as the proper domain for the gender expression of transpeople. Gavin Grimm, the Virginia teenager whose sued for the right to use the bathroom matching his gender identity, was told when he was barred from the boys' facilities at his school that he would be required to use a janitor's closet. A number of bills and ordinances passed at state and local levels require trans students to use "private" changing and showering facilities. Privacy, then, names a right that is being authored in order to allow cisgendered students to move through sex-segregated public spaces without any trans students present. The right to privacy means a right to public space purged of transpeople. And privacy, for trans students, means being publically outed as trans, and then being removed from that public space for being trans.

According to the February 22 letter, the difficulty with the prior guidelines is that they relied on an ambiguous definition of the word "sex." By way of contrast, it notes that "a federal district court in Texas held that the term 'sex' unambiguously refers to biological sex." Thus, the letter maintains that the Obama administration's deployment of the term "sex" was ambiguous but that sex itself is not, and that it is the restoration of "sex" to its prior status as uncontested and unambiguous that is the aim of the letter. One of the many confounding contradictions in the letter: if what is at issue is the biological sex of the person seeking entrance to the restroom, then that person would seem to be covered by Title IX, which ensures that individuals are not discriminated against on the basis of sex, but it is precisely that protection that the letter is revoking. Transgender people are, in essence, unsexed by this document. It is not just the bathroom from which they are being ejected—it is the category of sex itself. Within this horizon, there is no transgressing or traversing gender. Indeed, there appears to be no such thing as "gender" at all. There is only "biological sex," a bodily fact that cannot be disputed.

The stupidities of this position are manifest and many. One of the most glaring is how "biological sex" is defined in this document and in new legislation proposed in state and local governments around the country. In February of 2016, the South Dakota legislature approved a bill (later vetoed by the Republican governor) that would force public school students into the bathroom and locker room corresponding to their "biological sex," which the bill defines as "a person's chromosomes and anatomy as identified at birth." By claiming that sex is "biological sex," the letter seems to assert that sex is equal to genital shape. But note that this is not the advancement of a simple materialism that would conflate a person's sex with that person's genitals. The genitals to which it refers are the genitals of a newborn, genitals that may have no relation at all to one's current physical body. This is an understanding of "biological" that is almost entirely dematerialized from the phenomenology of the body, either in its appearance from the outside or in its feeling from the inside. In insisting that the letter on the birth certificate is the arbiter of sex, irrespective of one's genitals, sex becomes the property of a document rather than a body, a manoeuver that I have explored in detail elsewhere.[4]

The public pushback from trans activists and allies has already been vehement and thorough. Chase Strangio has recently written about the difficulties with the terms "male bodied" and "female bodied" in media coverage of trans people.[5] Janet Mock, in an opinion piece for the *New York Times* critiquing the new bathroom legislation, offered these observations: "When trans students are told that they cannot use public facilities, it doesn't only block them from the toilet—it also blocks them from public life. It tells them with every sneer, every blocked door, that we do not want to see them, that they should go hide and that ultimately they do not belong. When schools become hostile environments, students cannot turn to them."[6] Mock's piece points to the ways in which these anti-trans policies transform a once-welcoming space into a hostile one through exclusion, by sanctioning the exile of trans youth. The title of her piece, "Young People Get Trans Rights. It's Adults Who Don't," points to the generational divide on the question of trans rights. It also calls to mind Aliyah, the student at E. O. Green Junior High, who characterized Latisha's gender with more precision than any of the adults in the school or in the courtroom: "I don't think that Larry is gay, he's transgendered. It's a big difference."[7] As Mock emphasizes, the reach of anti-trans bathroom regulations are wider than just bathrooms; they are about the policing of trans bodies. This legal struggle is not about bathrooms any more than desegregation was about water fountains, lunch counters, or municipal buses. The point is to purge transpeople from public spaces. To make them disappear.

o o o

On February 23, the day after the Trump administration's Dear Colleague letter was released, MSNBC's *Hardball with Chris Matthews* hosted a panel discussion on the new anti-trans legislation, featuring actress Laverne Cox, Mara Kiesling from the National Center for Transgender

Equality, and Travis Weber from the Family Research Council. Matthews started by asking Weber which bathroom he thought Cox and Kiesling should use, if not the women's room? Weber refused to answer, dodging the question each of the half-dozen times Matthews posed it. Cox, like Janet Mock, pointed out that the issue was not about bathrooms and not about genitals, but about the right of trans people to exist in public space. "My transition," she said, "was about me existing in public space, and because I was able to do that I was able to thrive. That's all we want."

Weber then objected to the other panelists' discussion of trans rights, asserting that theirs were not the rights being abridged: "Whose rights are being overlooked here? The girls who are going into locker rooms." Weber was then challenged again by Matthews:

MATTHEWS: Who has standing on this, besides transgender people? Your side of the argument is that people are harmed by transgender people going into the bathroom they feel comfortable in. You say people are harmed by that. Who is harmed?

WEBER: Students in high schools.

MATTHEWS: Who is harmed?

WEBER: Students in high schools.

MATTHEWS: Describe them. What's the harm?

WEBER: I think we all understand what the harm is.

MATTHEWS: I don't.

WEBER: A fourteen-year-old girl in the locker room, someone comes in with male genitalia into their locker room, of course they are going to be harmed. Their rights are not being protected here.

We all understand what the harm is. Weber appeals to common sense, to what we all know, what we all understand. Common sense rallies in response to a shock, the shock of a trans woman in the women's restroom, a nonevent that is transformed into a shock through the coercions of common sense. It confidently asserts what "we all understand," an appeal both blatant and a dog-whistle, to fantasies of trans predation. Undeterred by Matthews's response that he does not understand what "we all" understand, and unresponsive to Matthews's demand for a phenomenological account of harm ("Describe them"), Weber trots out the myth, as false and outrageous as it is oft-repeated, of trans women representing a danger to cis girls. And, through this instant reversal, he transforms transpeople, who are overwhelmingly the victims of harassment and assault in bathrooms and other public spaces, into the agents of the violence, rather than its target. As the above exchange also shows, not all trans people are equally hailed and targeted by this new legislation. The threats whom these laws imagine are, for the most part, transwomen specifically, rather than transpeople in general. As Paisley Currah makes clear, the logic that trans women present a threat in a bathroom is just another iteration of the fear that they present a threat per se. This is a new resurrection of an old front for an old hatred, "trans panic" playing out in different terrain.[8]

Again and still, gender identity is read as a form of sexual behavior. Again and still, non-normative gender expression is conflated with sexual aggression. Like so many fantasies, this one conspires to bring about the thing that it most fears through its insistence that transpeople use the bathroom of the sex they were assigned at birth. In the guise of protecting girls from men in the women's room, the policy ejects (trans) women from the bathroom and forces (trans) men into that bathroom instead, insuring with one fell swoop that (trans) women will indeed be at heightened risk for harassment and violence in the mens' bathrooms to which they have been remanded and that (cis) women will now be sharing sex-segregated bathrooms with (trans) men. The policy is perfectly performative, bringing into existence exactly the situation—men in the women's room—that it purports to be solving. Again and still, it is mandating violence in the name of safety.

Transpeople—and trans children and young adults in particular—have indeed become more visible in the years since the killing of Latisha King. But what this new wave of anti-trans legislation demonstrates is that visibility is not in itself a sufficient condition to insure the protections of transpeople. Indeed, we can note the ways in which these bathroom bills are designed to disappear transpeople, but not before first rendering them hyper-visible. The current administration's address to the trans community is the precise inverse of Lynch's declaration of recognition and solidarity: *We will not see you, we will not stand with you, and we will do everything we can to strip you of protection going forward. You are retroactively crossed-out.*

ACKNOWLEDGMENTS

Ken Corbett was my daily and stalwart companion during every day of the trial and through much of the aftermath. I am grateful for his gentle presence and his kind heart. He is a model of how to listen, with compassion, to everyone. Judith Butler workshopped this material with both of us at a crucial stage, and this book is better for it. I am grateful for her support and for the legacy of her work.

During the trial I benefitted from conversations with Marta Cunningham, Kris Clarkin, Dan Swanson and Maeve Fox. I am grateful to Julie Salamon for fielding my late-night post-court phone calls and guiding me through each new day of legal puzzlement.

Ann Pellegrini has been a perfect editor: keen-eyed, encouraging, and remarkably patient. Thanks also to Eric Zinner and Lisha Nadkarni at New York University Press. I continue to rely on the quick and expert mind of Cathy Hannabach.

Thanks to my colleagues at Princeton University, especially Zahid Chaudhary, Jill Dolan, Reg Kunzel, Meredith Martin, Anne Cheng, Anne McClintock, Rob Nixon, Diana Fuss, Andrew Cole, Vance Smith, and Jeff Dolven. Thanks to Maria Papadakis for all-around wizardry. Thanks to the Queer Subcommittee for sanity-inducing scotch-o-clock.

Love to my California kin: Lila Thirkield, Armon Kasmai, Miss A, Dusty Jermier. Thanks to The Secrets of Family Happiness. Thanks to Weeble for always sharing the hedge and for stenography tape that graces the cover of this book. Thanks to Nello Carlini, who has taught me how to take the long view.

Gratitude to my wingfemme, Rebekah Edwards. Since I started writing this book, she has walked with me through every realm worth walking through, and even and especially through those that weren't—the sign of a true friend.

Thanks to Ann Murphy, my dear friend and phenomenological co-conspirator, with whom I always hope to keep rediscovering the magic of place.

For units and less-quantifiable companionate travels, I am grateful to Tey Meadow, Rebekah Edwards, David Kazanjian, A. B. Huber, Zahid Chaudhary, and Meredith Martin.

I am grateful to Joan Scott, for her intellectual curiosity and for cinematic escape. Thanks to Elizabeth Weed, who is my model for how to ask the right question.

Thanks to Sara Ahmed, Talia Bettcher, Cheryl Clark, Christina Crosby, Harry Dodge, Leigh Gilmore, Lisa Guenther, Samir Haddad, Cathy Hannabach, Cressida Heyes, Janet Jakobsen, Maggie Nelson, Sonia Olive, Lily Rodriguez, Rick Salamon, Avgi Saketopolou, Jill Stauffer, Sandy Stone, Susan Stryker, Bob Vallier, Willy Wilkerson, and Gail Weiss.

Gasshō to Issan Koyama, to Leslie James, to Linda Gallijan, to Teah Strozer, and to Greg Snyder. A pie-shake's worth of love to Doan Roessler. Katy Dion has been a true *mitra*. I thank Jody Greene for paths to practice. Mistake practice deserves its own altar in my life, and I am grateful to the outrageously talented Ella Marcantonio for giving me a beautiful place to reflect on it daily. Thank you to Yuko Okumura, for teaching me how to gather up all the pieces and make them into a patched whole. Deepest bows to Shohaku Okumura.

Red Robinson is the happiest person I know, and makes my life happier in innumerable ways. Greta Neunder is as badass a diesel femme as you will ever find. I am grateful to both of them beyond words, and proud to call them family.

I am grateful to Julie Salamon and Mike Travers, who gave me a place to start writing this book, and to Byron Kim and Lisa Sigal, who gave me a place to finish it.

Final thanks to Wing, Ann Murphy, David, Tey, Zahid, John, and Red, who helped me when I needed help. This book found its way back toward the world because of you. As did I.

A previous version of chapter 1 was published as "Passing Period" in Maaike Bleeker, Jon Foley Sherman, and Eirini Nedelkopoulou, eds., *Performance and Phenomenology: Traditions and Transformations* (New York: Routledge, Taylor & Francis, 2015).

NOTES

INTRODUCTION

1 All testimony from the trial comes from my own notes, except in those instances where I cite from the official transcript.

2 Bettcher, "When Selves Have Sex."

3 *People of the State of California vs. Brandon David McInerney*, case number 2008005782. Court reporter's transcript at 80-81. Testimony of Abiam M. July 7, 2011.

4 Phenomenology, of course, does not have exclusive methodological claim to the "how." For an insightful articulation of *how* versus *why* in trans studies, see Aizura's *Mobile Subjects*.

5 Merleau-Ponty, *In Praise of Philosophy*, 32–33.

6 Guenther, *Solitary Confinement: Social Death and Its Afterlives*, xiii, xv (emphasis in original).

7 For a Husserlian explication of critical phenomenology, see Aldea, "Phenomenology as Critique," particularly her explication of "hermeneutic patience." See also Dodd, *Crisis and Reflection*.

8 Zaner, *The Way of Phenomenology*, 202.

9 Ahmed, *Queer Phenomenology*, 103.

10 Morrison, *Playing in the Dark*.

11 Best, "The Fear of Black Bodies in Motion."

12 Sheth, *Toward a Political Philosophy of Race*, 66, 68.

13 Snorton and Haritaworn, "Trans Necropolitics," 69.

14 On violence, ontology, and queer and trans lives of color, see Stanley, "Near Life, Queer Death." See also Hayward, "Don't Exist."

15 Marriott, *On Black Men*, viii.

16 Stryker, *Transgender History*, 19.

CHAPTER 1. COMPORTMENT

1 Hernandez, "Judge Rules Teen Accused of Murder May Switch Lawyers."

2 Foxman, "McInerney Dealt a Setback by Ventura Court."

3 Hernandez, "Jury selection will begin Nov. 15 in McInerney murder trial."

4 Boldrin, court reporter's transcript, July 8, 2011, 9.

5 Boldrin, court reporter's transcript, July 8, 2011, 26.

6 Boldrin, court reporter's transcript, July 8, 2011, 30.

7 Corbett, *Boyhoods*, 195.

8 Corbett, *Boyhoods*, 196.

9 Hernandez, "Days before Trial, McInerney Attorneys Say They Have No Defense."

10 Hernandez, Raul. "School Shooting Described at McInerney Hearing."

11 Husserl, *Ideas* 1 S75, p. 167.

12 Straus, "The Upright Posture," 244.

13 Straus, "The Upright Posture," 232.

14 Straus, "The Upright Posture," 232.

15 Straus, "The Upright Posture," 232.

16 Straus, "The Upright Posture," 232.

17 Straus, "The Upright Posture," 233.

18 Straus, "The Upright Posture," 233.

19 Straus, "The Upright Posture," 233.

20 Straus, "The Upright Posture," 235.

21 Straus, "The Upright Posture," 234.

22 Straus, "The Upright Posture," 236.

23 Of course, such a conflation of uprightness with human-ness can have pernicious implications. For a consideration of Straus from a critical disability perspective, see Abrams, "Is Everyone Upright?"

24 Straus, "The Upright Posture," 236.

25 Straus, "The Upright Posture," 239.

26 Straus, "The Upright Posture," 238.

27 Straus, "The Upright Posture," 240.

28 Straus, "The Upright Posture," 241.

29 Straus, "The Upright Posture," 241.

30 Rodriguez, *Sexual Futures, Queer Gestures, and Other Latina Longings*, 103.

31 Straus, 241. In a footnote to this comment, Straus notes that "the root is Latin, *clino*, to bend. It is interesting to see how

greatly language is shaped in accordance with expressive phenomena."

32 Welch, "Homosexuality in America," 70.

33 Welch, "Homosexuality in America."

34 Sinclair, court reporter's transcript, 52–53.

35 Sinclair, court reporter's transcript, 13.

36 Welch, "Homosexuality in America."

37 See Salamon, "Humiliation and Transgender Regulation."

CHAPTER 2. MOVEMENT

1 Moten, *In the Break*, 200.

2 Moten, *In the Break*, 192.

3 Schütz, *Collected Papers*, 1:232.

4 Natanson, *Anonymity*, 78.

5 Zaner, *The Way of Phenomenology*, 43.

6 Merleau-Ponty, "Indirect Language and the Voices of Silence," x (emphasis mine).

7 This is Michael B. Smith's choice in the translation in the *Merleau-Ponty Aesthetics Reader*.

8 Richard McCleary's English translation in *Signs*.

9 Merleau-Ponty, "Indirect Language and the Voices of Silence," 112.

10 Merleau-Ponty, "Indirect Language and the Voices of Silence,"117.

11 Sinclair, court reporter's transcript, 16.

12 Sinclair, court reporter's transcript, 24.

13 Sinclair, court reporter's transcript, 57–58.

14 Sinclair, court reporter's transcript, 58–60.

15 Sinclair, court reporter's transcript, 47–48.

16 Weiss, *Refiguring the Ordinary*, 20.

17 Merleau-Ponty, *The Visible and the Invisible*, 155.

18 Merleau-Ponty, "Indirect Language and the Voices of Silence," 79.

19 Merleau-Ponty, "Indirect Language and the Voices of Silence," 79.

20 Johnson, "Structures and Painting," 27.

21 Merleau-Ponty, "Indirect Language and the Voices of Silence," 82.

22 Merleau-Ponty, "Indirect Language and the Voices of Silence," 105.

23 In *Our Word is Our Bond*, Marianne Constable understands law to be a matter of language (rather than merely statutes or rules), and also suggests that one of its tasks is negotiating failures of language. "Law acts through persuading hearers," she writes. In this case, we can see the persuasive force of the legal argument made through acts of language that are eloquent and effective, even as they are wordless. See Constable, *Our Word is Our Bond*, 134.

24 Obama, "Remarks by the President on Trayvon Martin."

25 Yancy, *Black Bodies, White Gazes*, xix.

26 Harney and Moten's *The Undercommons* opens with a description, writ large, of the projection of aggression onto the aggressed by the aggressor: "In Michael Parenti's classic anti-imperial analysis of Hollywood movies, he points to the 'upside down' way that the 'make-believe media' portrays colonial settlement. In films like *Drums along the Mohawk* (1939) or *Shaka Zulu* (1987), the settler is portrayed as surrounded by 'natives,' inverting, in Parenti's view, the role of aggressor so that colonialism is made to look like self-defense. Indeed, aggression and self-defense are reversed in these movies, but the image of a surrounded fort is not false. Instead, the false image is what emerges when a critique of militarised life is predicated on the forgetting of the life that surrounds it. The fort really was surrounded, is besieged by what still surrounds it, the common beyond and beneath—before and before—enclosure. The surround antagonises the laager in its midst while disturbing that facts on the ground with some outlaw planning." (17).

27 King, *The Riot Within*, 226.

28 Weiss, *Refiguring the Ordinary*, 102.

29 Gooding-Williams, *Reading Rodney King*.

30 Freud, "Contributions to a Discussion on Suicide," 231–232.

31 Freud, "Contributions to a Discussion on Suicide," 231–232 (emphasis in original).

32 Segwick, "Queer and Now," 1.

33 Sedgwick, "Queer and Now," 2 (emphasis in original).

34 See Puar, "Coda: The Cost of Getting Better."

35 Rose, "Deadly Embrace," 21.

CHAPTER 3. ANONYMITY

1 Reynolds, "Maurice Merleau-Ponty," 3.
2 See Halpin, "The Philosophy of Anonymous."
3 Cited in Natanson, *Anonymity*, 21.
4 Beauvoir, *The Ethics of Ambiguity*.
5 Though Beauvoir has historically been categorized as an existentialist, recent scholarship has traced the conceptual and historical importance of phenomenology to her work. On this question, and on the matter of Merleau-Ponty's and Beauvoir's shared commitment to ambiguity, see Weiss, "Beauvoir and Merleau-Ponty." On Beauvoir's relationship to Merleau-Ponty, and his indebtedness to some of her formulations, see also McWeeny, "The Feminist Phenomenology of Excess."
6 Natanson, *Anonymity*, 150.
7 Natanson, *Anonymity*, 92.
8 Lawlor, *Early Twentieth-Century Continental Philosophy*, 3.
9 Schütz, *The Phenomenology of the Social World*, 77.
10 Natanson, *Anonymity*, 101.
11 Natanson, *Anonymity*, 100.
12 Natanson, *Anonymity*, 107.
13 Natanson, *Anonymity*, 107.
14 Zaner, *The Way of Phenomenology*, 49.
15 Natanson, *Anonymity*, 83.
16 Zaner, *The Way of Phenomenology*, 50 (emphasis in original).
17 On the matter of the sidewaysness of the queer child's temporality, see Stockton, *The Queer Child*. On the matter of temporality and queerness more broadly, see Halberstam, *In a Queer Time and Place*, and Freeman, *Time Binds*.
18 On the matter of "anonymous life" as a mode of retreat from relation in *Phenomenology of Perception*, see my "The Place Where Life Hides Away."
19 Merleau-Ponty, *Phenomenology of Perception*, 347.
20 Merleau-Ponty, *Phenomenology of Perception*, 215.
21 Merleau-Ponty, *Phenomenology of Perception*, 312.
22 Merleau-Ponty, *Phenomenology of Perception*, 238.
23 Merleau-Ponty, *Phenomenology of Perception*, 348.

24 See Merleau-Ponty, *Phenomenology of Perception*, 351.

25 Merleau-Ponty, *Phenomenology of Perception*, 352.

26 Merleau-Ponty, *Phenomenology of Perception*, 352.

27 Stoller, "Gender and Anonymous Temporality," 85.

28 Heinamaa, "Personality, Anonymity and Sexual Difference," 42.

29 Heinamaa, "Personality, Anonymity and Sexual Difference," 42 (emphasis in original).

30 Heinamaa, "Personality, Anonymity and Sexual Difference," 46.

31 See in particular "Cezanne's Doubt" in *The Merleau-Ponty Aesthetics Reader* and "Indirect Languages and the Voices of Silence" for a discussion of style as a description of bodily practice and its relation to meaning.

32 Schütz, cited in Natanson, *Anonymity*, 100.

CHAPTER 4. OBJECTS

1 Andrea V., court reporter's transcript, 69–70.

2 Merleau-Ponty, *Phenomenology of Perception*, 319.

3 Boldrin, court reporter's transcript, July 28, 2011, 96.

4 Boldrin, court reporter's transcript, July 28, 2011, 96.

5 Boldrin, court reporter's transcript, July 28, 2011, 97.

6 Boldrin, court reporter's transcript, July 28, 2011, 98.

7 Cunningham, *Valentine Road*.

8 On boys' conceptions of bigness and smallness in the clinical scene and the relation of size to masculinity and sexuality, see "Faggot/Loser" in Ken Corbett's *Boyhoods*.

9 For Plato, such determinations were crucial not just for everyday living, but also to the integrity of the social fabric. Recall that one of the reasons he wanted to banish poets from the republic is because poetry works by "gratifying our irrational side, which can't even recognize what size things are. An object which at one moment it calls big, it might call small the next moment." Plato, *Republic, 605b*.

10 Merleau-Ponty, *Sorbonne*, 192 (emphasis in original).

11 On Husserlian ethics, see Tom Nenon's review of *Husserliana* 28, "Husserl's Ethics?," Peuker, "From Logic to Person," Ferrarello, *Husserl's Ethics and Practical Intentionality*, and Siles i Borràs, *The Ethics of Husserl's Phenomenology*.

12 Drummond, "Phenomenology, Eudaimonia, and the Virtues," 97. See also Drummond and Embree, *Phenomenological Approaches to Moral Philosophy.*

13 Marx, *Towards a Phenomenological Ethics*, 33 (emphasis in original).

14 Marx, *Towards a Phenomenological Ethics*, 33.

15 Cunningham, *Valentine Road.*

16 Elsewhere, I analyze a civil suit filed by Latisha's parents after her death but prior to the criminal trial and observe that it was her improper affect as much as her transgressive gender that was targeted by her schoolmates and her parents. I argue there that "Larry becomes a target not just because he violates gender norms but because he does so without a sufficient sense of shame. See Salamon, "Humiliation and Transgender Regulation."

17 Husserl, *Analyses Concerning Passive and Active Synthesis.*

18 Cunningham, *Valentine Road.*

CODA

1 Wolff, "The Ugly Fantasy at the Heart of Anti-Trans Bathroom Bills."

2 DeVos was reported to have had "misgivings" about the policy. Mead, "Betsy DeVos's Spineless Transgender Bathroom Politics."

3 Lynch, "Attorney General Loretta E. Lynch Delivers Remarks."

4 See my "Withholding the Letter" in *Assuming a Body.*

5 Strangio, "What Is a 'Male Body'?"

6 Mock, "Janet Mock: Young People Get Trans Rights.

7 Cunningham, *Valentine Road.*

8 Currah, "The New Transgender Panic." For a thorough analysis, see also his forthcoming book, *Not the United States of Sex: Sex Classification and Transgender Politics* (New York University Press).

WORKS CITED

Abrams, Thomas. "Is Everyone Upright? Erwin Straus' 'The Upright Posture' and Disabled Phenomenology." *Human Affairs* 24, no. 4 (2014): 564–573.

Ahmed, Sara. *Queer Phenomenology: Orientations, Objects, Others.* Durham, NC: Duke University Press, 2006.

Aizura, Aren. *Mobile Subjects: Transnational Imaginaries of Gender Reassignment.* Durham, NC: Duke University Press, 2018.

Aldea, Andreea Smaranda. "Phenomenology as Critique: Teleological-Historical Reflection and Husserl's Transcendental Eidetics." *Husserl Studies* 32, no. 1 (2016): 21–46.

Beauvoir, Simone de. *The Ethics of Ambiguity.* New York: Kensington, 1976.

Benjamin, Jessica. *The Bonds of Love: Psychoanalysis, Feminism, and the Problem of Domination.* New York: Pantheon, 1988.

Best, Wallace. "The Fear of Black Bodies in Motion." *Huffington Post*, February 3, 2015. www.huffingtonpost.com.

Bettcher, Talia. "When Selves Have Sex: What the Phenomenology of Trans Sexuality Can Teach about Sexual Orientation." *Journal of Homosexuality* 61, no. 5 (2014): 605–20.

Bond, Justin. "Justin Vivian Bond: Childhood, Revisited." Interview by Robert Smith, *Lambda Literary*, September 12, 2011. www.lambdaliterary.org.

———. *Tango: My Childhood, Backwards and in High Heels.* New York: Feminist Press, 2011.

Butler, Judith. "Endangered/Endangering: Schematic Racism and White Paranoia." In *Reading Rodney King/Reading Urban Uprising*, edited by Robert Gooding-Williams. New York: Routledge, 1993.

Cairns, Dorion. "An Approach to Phenomenology." In *Essays in Memory of Edmund Husserl*, edited by Martin Farber. Cambridge, MA: Harvard University Press, 1940.

Constable, Marianne. *Our Word is Our Bond: How Legal Speech Acts.* Stanford: Stanford University Press, 2014.

Corbett, Ken. *A Murder over a Girl: Justice, Gender, Junior High.* New York: Henry Holt, 2016.

———. *Boyhoods: Rethinking Masculinities.* New Haven, CT: Yale University Press, 2009.

Cunningham, Marta. *Valentine Road.* DVD. Directed by Marta Cunningham. HBO Docs/BMP Films, 2013.

Currah, Paisley. "The New Transgender Panic: Men in Women's Bathrooms." *Paisley Currah*, March 31, 2016. www.paisleycurrah.com.

Dillon, M. C. *Merleau-Ponty's Ontology.* Bloomington: Indiana University Press, 1988.

Dodd, J. *Crisis and Reflection. An Essay on Husserl's Crisis of the European Sciences.* Dordrecht: Kluwer, 2004.

Drummond, "Phenomenology, Eudaimonia, and the Virtues." In *Phenomenology and Virtue Ethics,* edited by Kevin Hermberg and Paul Gyllenhammer. London: Bloomsbury, 2015.

Edelman, Lee. *No Future: Queer Theory and the Death Drive.* Durham, NC: Duke University Press, 2004.

Embree, Lester E., and J. J. Drumond, eds. *Phenomenological Approaches to Moral Philosophy: A Handbook.* Dordrecht: Springer Netherlands, 2002.

Ferrarello, Susi. *Husserl's Ethics and Practical Intentionality.* London: Bloomsbury, 2016.

Foxman, Adam. "McInerney Dealt a Setback by Ventura Court." *Ventura County Star,* November 6, 2009.

Freeman, Elizabeth. *Time Binds: Queer Temporalities, Queer Histories.* Durham, NC: Duke University Press, 2010.

Freud, Sigmund. "Contributions to a Discussion on Suicide" (1910). In *The Standard Edition of the Complete Psychological Works of Sigmund Freud,* edited and translated by James Strachey, vol. 11. London: The Hogarth Press, 1953–1974.

Gooding-Williams, Robert. *Reading Rodney King: Reading Urban Uprising.* New York: Routledge, 1993.

Guenther, Lisa. *Solitary Confinement: Social Death and Its Afterlives.* Minneapolis: University of Minnesota Press, 2013.

Halberstam, Judith. *In a Queer Time and Place: Transgender Bodies, Subcultural Lives.* New York: New York University Press, 2005.

Halpin, Harry. "The Philosophy of Anonymous: Ontological Politics without Identity." *Radical Philosophy* 176 (November–December 2012): 19–28.

Harney, Stefano, and Fred Moten. *The Undercommons: Fugitive Planning and Black Study*. Minor Compositions, 2013.

Hayward, Eva. "Don't Exist." *TSQ* 4, no. 2 (2017): 191–194.

Heinamaa, Sara. *Toward a Phenomenology of Sexual Difference: Husserl, Merleau-Ponty, Beauvoir*. Lanham, MD: Rowman & Littlefield, 2003.

———. "Personality, Anonymity and Sexual Difference." In *Time in Feminist Phenomenology*, edited by Christina Schues, Dorothea Olkowski, and Helen Fielding. Bloomington: Indiana University Press, 2011.

Hermberg, Kevin, and Paul Gyllenhammer, eds. *Phenomenology and Virtue Ethics*. London: Bloomsbury, 2013.

Hernandez, Raul. "Jury Selection Will Begin Nov. 15 in McInerney Murder Trial." *Ventura County Star*, September 9, 2010.

———. "Days before Trial, McInerney Attorneys Say They Have No Defense." *Ventura County Star*, July 14, 2010.

———. "School Shooting Described at McInerney Hearing." *Ventura County Star*, July 21, 2009.

———. "Judge Rules Teen Accused of Murder May Switch Lawyers." *Ventura County Star*, October 15, 2008.

Husserl, Edmund. *Analyses Concerning Passive and Active Synthesis*. Translated by Anthony J. Steinbock. Dordrecht: Kluwer Academic, 2001.

———. *Ideas Pertaining to a Pure Phenomenology and to a Phenomenological Philosophy*. Dordrecht: Kluwer, 1982.

Husserl, Edmund, and Marvin Farber. *Philosophical Essays in Memory of Edmund Husserl*. New York: Greenwood Press, 1968.

Johnson, Galen A. "Structures and Painting." In *The Merleau-Ponty Aesthetics Reader: Philosophy and Painting*. Evanston, IL: Northwestern University Press, 1993.

Kersten, Fred, and Richard M. Zaner. *Phenomenology: Continuation and Criticism; Essays in Memory of Dorion Cairns*. The Hague: M. Nijhoff, 1973.

King, Rodney. *The Riot Within: My Journey from Rebellion to Redemption*. New York: Harper Collins, 2012.

Lawlor, Leonard. *Early Twentieth-Century Continental Philosophy*. Bloomington: Indiana University Press, 2012.

Lynch, Loretta E. "Attorney General Loretta E. Lynch Delivers Remarks at Press Conference Announcing Complaint against the State of North Carolina to Stop Discrimination against Transgender Individuals." United States Department of Justice, May 9, 2016. www.justice.gov.

Marriott, David. *On Black Men*. New York: Columbia University Press, 2000.

Marx, Werner. *Towards a Phenomenological Ethics: Ethos and the Life-World*. Albany: State University of New York Press, 1992.

McWeeny, Jen. "The Feminist Phenomenology of Excess: Ontological Multiplicity, Auto-Jealousy, and Suicide in Beauvoir's *L'Invitée*." *Continental Philosophy Review* 45, no. 1 (2012): 41–75.

Mead, Rebecca. "Betsy Devos's Spineless Transgender Bathroom Politics." *New Yorker*, February 23, 2017. www.newyorker.com.

Merleau-Ponty, Maurice. *Child Psychology and Pedagogy: The Sorbonne Lectures 1949–1952*. Translated by Talia Welsh. Northwestern University Press, 2010.

———. *Phenomenology of Perception*. Translated by Colin Smith. London: Routledge, 2002.

———. *Husserl at the Limits of Phenomenology*. Edited by Leonard Lawlor and Bettina Bergo. Evanston, IL: Northwestern University Press, 2002.

———. *The Visible and the Invisible*. Translated by Alphonso Lingis. Evanston, IL: Northwestern University Press, 1968.

———. "Indirect Language and the Voices of Silence." In *Signs*. Translated by Richard McCleary. Evanston, IL: Northwestern University Press, 1964.

———. *In Praise of Philosophy*. Evanston, IL: Northwestern University Press, 1963.

Merleau-Ponty, Maurice, Johnson, Galen A., and Michael B. Smith. *The Merleau-Ponty Aesthetics Reader: Philosophy and Painting*. Evanston, IL: Northwestern University Press, 1993.

Mock, Janet. "Janet Mock: Young People Get Trans Rights. It's Adults Who Don't." *New York Times*, February 23, 2017. www.nytimes.com.

Morrison, Toni. *Playing in the Dark: Whiteness and the Literary Imagination*. New York: Vintage Books, 1992.

Moten, Fred. *In the Break: The Aesthetics of the Black Radical Tradition*. Minneapolis: University of Minnesota Press, 2003.

Muñoz, José Esteban. *Cruising Utopia: The Then and There of Queer Futurity*. New York: New York University Press, 2009.

Natanson, Maurice Alexander. *Anonymity: A Study in the Philosophy of Alfred Schütz*. Bloomington: Indiana University Press, 1986.

Nenon, Tom. "Husserl's Ethics?" *Research in Phenomenology* 20.1 (1990): 184-188.

Obama, Barack. "Remarks by the President on Trayvon Martin." July 19, 2013. Obama White House Archives. www.obamawhitehouse.archives.gov.

People of the State of California vs. Brandon David McInerney, Docket No. 2008005782. Court reporter's transcript: Testimony of Abiam M: July 7, 2011. Testimony of Anne Sinclair: July 29, 2011. Testimony of Dawn Boldrin: Friday, July 8, 2011, Monday, July 11, 2011, Thursday, July 28, 2011, Friday, July 29, 2011. Testimony of Andrea V. July 7, 2011.

Peucker, Henning. "From Logic to the Person: An Introduction to Edmund Husserl's Ethics." *Review of Metaphysics* 62, no. 2 (2008): 307–325.

Plato. *The Republic*. Translated by Benjamin Jowett. Amherst, NY: Prometheus Books, 1988.

Puar, Jasbir. "Coda: The Cost of Getting Better." *GLQ: A Journal of Lesbian and Gay Studies* 18, no. 1 (2012): 149–158.

Reynolds, Jack. "Maurice Merleau-Ponty: Life and Works." In *Merleau-Ponty: Key Concepts*, edited by Jack Reynolds and Ros Diprose. London: Acumen, 2008.

Rodríguez, Juana María. *Sexual Futures, Queer Gestures, and Other Latina Longings*. New York: New York University Press, 2014.

Rose, Jacqueline. "Deadly Embrace." *London Review of Books* 26, no. 21 (2004): 21–24.

Salamon, Gayle. *Assuming a Body: Transgender and Rhetorics of Materiality*. New York: Columbia University Press, 2010.

———. "Humiliation and Transgender Regulation: Reply to Ken Corbett." *Psychoanalytic Dialogues* 19, no. 4 (2009): 376–84.

———. "The Place Where Life Hides Away: Merleau-Ponty, Fanon, and the Location of Bodily Being." *differences* 17, no. 2 (2006): 96–111.

Schütz, Alfred. *The Phenomenology of the Social World*. Evanston, IL: Northwestern University Press, 1967.

———. *Collected Papers*. The Hague: Nijhoff, 1966.

Schütz, Alfred, and Maurice Alexander Natanson, ed. *Phenomenology and Social Reality; Essays In Memory of Alfred Schutz*. The Hague: Nijhoff, 1970.

Sedgwick, Eve Kosofsky. *Touching Feeling: Affect, Performativity, Pedagogy*. Durham, NC: Duke University Press, 2003.

———. "Queer and Now." In *Tendencies*. Durham, NC: Duke University Press, 1993.

Setoodeh, Ramin. "Young, Gay, and Murdered in Junior High." *Newsweek*, July 28, 2008. www.newsweek.com.

Sheth, Falguni. *Toward a Political Philosophy of Race*. Albany: SUNY Press, 2009.

Siles i Borràs, Joaquim. *The Ethics of Husserl's Phenomenology: Responsibility and Ethical Life*. London: Bloomsbury, 2010.

Snorton, C. Riley, and Jin Haritaworn. "Trans Necropolitics: A Transnational Reflection on Violence, Death, and the Trans of Color Afterlife." *Transgender Studies Reader* 2 (2013): 66–76.

Stanley, Eric. "Near Life, Queer Death: Overkill and Ontological Capture." *Social Text*, no. 107. (2011): 1–19.

Stockton, Kathryn Bond. *The Queer Child, or Growing Sideways in the Twentieth Century*. Durham, NC: Duke University Press, 2009.

Stoller, Sylvia. "Gender and Anonymous Temporality." In *Time in Feminist Phenomenology*, edited by Christina Schues, Dorothea Olkowski, and Helen Fielding. Bloomington: Indiana University Press, 2011.

Straus, Erwin. "The Upright Posture." In *Phenomenology and Existentialism*, edited by Richard Zaner and Don Ihde. New York: Capricorn, 1973.

———. *Phenomenological Psychology: The Selected Papers of Erwin W. Straus*. Translated, in part, by Erling Eng. New York: Basic Books, 1966.

Strangio, Chase. "What Is a 'Male Body'?" *Slate*, July 19, 2016. www.slate.com.

Stryker, Susan. *Transgender History*. Berkeley, CA: Seal Press, 2008.

Weiss, Gail. "Beauvoir and Merleau-Ponty: Philosophers of Ambiguity." In *Beauvoir Engages Philosophy: Essays on Beauvoir's Dialogue with Western Thought*, edited by Shannon Mussett and William A. Wilkerson. Albany: State University of New York Press, 2012.

———. *Refiguring the Ordinary*. Bloomington: Indiana University Press, 2008.

Welch, Paul. "Homosexuality in America." *Life* 56, no. 26 (June 26, 1964): 66–74, 76–80.

Wolff, Tobias. "The Ugly Fantasy at the Heart of Anti-Trans Bathroom Bills." *Nation*, March 25, 2016. www.thenation.com.

Yancy, George, and Janine Jones, eds. *Pursuing Trayvon Martin: Historical Contexts and Contemporary Manifestations of Racial Dynamics*. Lanham, MD: Lexington Books, 2014.

Yancy, George. *Black Bodies, White Gazes: The Continuing Significance of Race*. Lanham, MD: Rowman & Littlefield, 2008.

Young, Iris Marion. *Throwing Like a Girl and Other Essays*. Bloomington: Indiana University Press, 1990.

Zadjermann, Paule, dir. *Judith Butler: Philosophical Encounters of the Third Kind*. Arte, 2006.

Zaner, Richard M. *The Way of Phenomenology: Criticism as a Philosophical Discipline*. New York: Pegasus, 1970.

———. *The Problem of Embodiment: Some Contributions to a Phenomenology of the Body*. The Hague: Nijhoff, 1964.

INDEX

ABOUT THE AUTHOR

Gayle Salamon is Professor of English and Gender and Sexuality Studies at Princeton University. Her research interests include phenomenology, feminist philosophy, queer and transgender theory, psychoanalysis, visual culture, and disability studies. She lives in Brooklyn.

For a complete list of books in the series, see www.nyupress.org